ॐ

Gift Ecology

gift
ECOLOGY

ॐ

Reimagining a
Sustainable
World

PETER DENTON

RMB
Victoria Vancouver Calgary

Rocky Mountain Books
www.rmbooks.com

Library and Archives Canada Cataloguing in Publication

Denton, Peter Harvey, 1959-
    Gift ecology : reimagining a sustainable world / Peter Denton.

Includes bibliographical references.
Issued also in electronic format.
ISBN 978-1-927330-41-8 (HTML).—ISBN 978-1-927330-48-7 (PDF)
ISBN 978-1-927330-40-1 (bound)

    1. Sustainability. 2. Human ecology. 3. Environmental economics. I. Title.

HC79.E5D4533 2012   338.9'27   C2012-903850-4

Printed and bound in Canada

Rocky Mountain Books acknowledges the financial support for its publishing program from the Government of Canada through the Canada Book Fund (CBF) and the province of British Columbia through the British Columbia Arts Council and the Book Publishing Tax Credit.

Canadian Heritage   Patrimoine canadien   Canada Council for the Arts   Conseil des Arts du Canada

BRITISH COLUMBIA ARTS COUNCIL
Supported by the Province of British Columbia

The interior pages of this book have been produced on 100% post-consumer recycled paper, processed chlorine free and printed with vegetable-based dyes.

MIX
Paper from responsible sources
FSC® C016245

ۀ
Contents

Preface

This book deals with the spaces in-between – between where we were and where we are, between where we are and where we could be – that are framed by the time of our lives.

Time is the most enigmatic of gifts. We seem to have it in abundance, until there is none of it left. It can be captured only through the impossible pretence of stepping outside of its stream. In a universe of relations, however, the intensity of a feeling is not measured by its duration, nor is the significance of a relationship something for clocks to account. It is all a matter of Presence.

In too rare moments of Presence, we encounter something that cannot be explained, only treasured, and find our universe is forever changed. Strangers instantly become friends and companions for life. Time outside the moment of that experience ceases to matter. Any ensuing separation becomes almost trivial, reflecting only the mereness of space.

At other moments of Presence, we are alone with a revelation of the universe in which we live. The epiphany is not about relationships with other people, but comes from turning our focus beyond the directions of the compass to one of the three additional directions that indigenous cultures have long affirmed:

We look up, and encounter the Creator or Source of the universe and all the life and possibilities within it. We look down, and encounter the Earth on which we stand and within whose life we are inescapably entwined. We look inside, and in a moment of self-recognition, encounter the essence of what truly lies in our hearts.

For those of you who understand what I mean, nothing more needs to be said. For the rest, may this short book give you something to think about, something to anticipate in everything you encounter, until you too experience what all of life is a quest to discover.

The reflections and the arguments that follow have emerged from the dynamic of engaging with the ideas of many people. I am thankful for the profligacy of my teachers, who shared their thoughts and feelings with students who, like me, only learned long afterward the value of the gifts they had been so freely given. For those of my own students who have listened, often wide-eyed, to impassioned lectures intended to broaden horizons they did not yet realize were there, I am grateful for your tolerance. I hope someday that you too will appreciate the gifts I have tried to give you. "The Bookshelf" provides a short narrative bibliography arranged by theme, including references for the authors whose ideas are referred to in various places throughout.

But for the encouragement of old friends and the enthusiasm of new ones, I would not have started the blog that led to this book, nor had the temerity to propose to Rocky Mountain Books that what I was writing should be published. I am thankful for the brief conversation I had with Bob Sandford at a conference last year, through which I was introduced to his colleague, Merrell-Ann Phare, to the Manifesto series in which their excellent books appeared, and thus to the people at RMB. I am especially grateful to RMB publisher Don Gorman for his willingness to see wisdom in my presumption. For everyone who has prodded me over the past fifteen years to publish more of what I have been teaching, I hope what you read here will have been worth the wait.

This book is dedicated to the memory of Wendy Siewert (1958–98). She was never able to write the books she intended, but her friendship and thoughtful generosity wrote pages in the lives of many other people, including my own.

Peter Denton
Winnipeg, Canada
April 2012

ॐ

The Argument

As the Earth lurches toward 2050, the chorus of conflicting voices grows louder and more confused: do we live on a planet in crisis or a planet in transition? Many see evidence of impending natural disaster driven by climate change and overpopulation. Others live toward a delightful but implausible futuristic world created and fuelled by human ingenuity.

In the first case, the analysis of numbers leads to the paralysis of despair. Nothing can be done to avert disaster, so there is little point in trying to change the way things are. In the second case, naive optimism leads to the inactivity of denial. Something needs to be done to change our impact on the planet, but not right away – and certainly not by us.

Neither option is helpful or hopeful. Both sidestep the necessity of knowing how our current situation was created, because such understanding is pointless in the first instance and irrelevant in the second. If we are headed for inevitable disaster, then it doesn't matter where it all began. If no disaster looms, just a bright and promising future, then brooding over the past just seems depressive.

As a result, neither doom nor denial enables us to make better choices toward a sustainable future. Most of us live in the uncertain space between these two conclusions, needing advice on which way to go and reassurance that our sacrifices are not futile gestures, yet finding neither.

This book tries to offer advice as well as reassurance, but it is grounded in the conviction that major changes are required in all of our lives. It is clear to me that a sustainable future is impossible unless we significantly alter the trajectory of how we live together – and soon. To do this, we must understand how the systems within which we live have shaped our present; without that understanding, we can't change how they will otherwise go on to shape our future.

Our problems with achieving sustainability are neither scientific nor technological. There is no "knowledge gap" that some new insight or discovery is needed to fill. We have all the science and technology we need, right now, to make the changes we need to create a sustainable future. We know what needs to be done. We even know how to do it. We just don't.

Sustainability is therefore a social and cultural problem, first and foremost. A sustainable future requires changes in how and why we live together. These changes, in their turn, will lead to the appropriate scientific, technological and environmental choices required for a sustainable global society.

The fault is not in our stars, nor in our tools. It is in ourselves, as citizens of the twenty-first century. To put it another way, the key issue is neither scientific inadequacy nor technological insufficiency. It is ethical incapacity. We are making consistently poor choices, both as individuals and as members of a global society. If we don't learn to make better choices today than we did yesterday, tomorrow will be bleak for those left to experience it.

In 1928, an American named Raymond Blaine Fosdick published *The Old Savage in the New Civilization,* a book that came out of a series of college commencement addresses. Appointed an Undersecretary General to the failed League of Nations, Fosdick argued that moral development had not kept pace with technological development. We were still the same Old Savage, now living in a New Civilization with tools capable of worldwide devastation. If we did not figure how to use these tools more wisely, he said, then the consequences for everyone would be catastrophic.

It was not unusual for books in the 1920s to reflect on the aftermath of the Great War of 1914–18, which in such a short space of time saw four empires destroyed and two more damaged beyond repair. Published at the height of the Roaring Twenties, Fosdick's book still must have seemed out of step – at least for a year, until the Crash of 1929, followed by the Depression, the rise of fascism and another world war that ushered in even more destructive weapons, culminating in the first use of the atomic bomb.

Fosdick did what he could to push the Old Savage in the right direction. From 1936 to 1948, he was president of the Rockefeller Foundation as it shifted its funding from the physical to the social sciences, looking for ways to socialize the

Old Savage into the New Civilization before it was too late.

More than eighty years after his book appeared, Fosdick's observations and concerns remain cogent. Our problem is not our tools; it is our ideas, our values, our attitudes.

The rapid environmental devastation caused by how we live can be slowed and reversed with the necessary changes to lifestyle and a concerted, collective effort.

Without a similar change in how we live together, however, the future is bleak. The problems inherent in our global socio-political system, combined with climate change and competition for dwindling resources on a crowded planet, will make further conflict inevitable. We need to find new ways to live together if we are to avoid the devastation that Fosdick feared.

There needs to be a social and cultural transformation, at all levels. We can legislate, berate and punish people into a sustainable lifestyle, but that isn't transformation – that's just coercion. We can pine for an earlier, idyllic time that will never return (and likely never existed anyway), but that just leads to paralysis. When individuals

make better choices every day, it leads to transformation. In those thoughtful, deliberate and
entirely personal choices, there is real hope.

Our choices, however, need to reverse some
trends that have increasingly dominated western
European society and then global society for the
past four hundred years. These trends have led to
an imbalance in how we live together with each
other and with the planet. They are encapsulated
by the exchange economy and the attitudes and
values it entails.

Locally, globally, even personally, it is disconcert-
ing to realize how much of life in the twenty-first
century is directed by the necessity of exchange.
We trade, we barter, we buy, we sell – in everything
we do there is an exchange, something offered and
expected in return. We live in a world of quid pro
quo, of something for something. We object to the
idea of getting nothing for something – though
we are happy to get something for nothing!

Contrary to what critics of consumerism say,
it is not just about the money. The expectation
of exchange is embedded in twenty-first century society in ways that go beyond any financial

transaction. "What's in it for me?" is a cruder version of this attitude, but not by much. Exchange requires a transaction between two parties, each of whom has something the other wants. Sometimes that transaction takes the form of barter, where different items are exchanged or some goods are exchanged for a service. Most often, what each side has to contribute to the transaction is valued in terms of a third element, usually money, which becomes the medium of exchange.

Social complexity follows very quickly, because we earn money for doing something in one part of our lives, only to spend it to acquire goods or services in another. The more people there are, the more transactions and the greater the complexity, to the point that now our transactions – our exchange economy – tie people together around the world. This, we are told, creates wealth and a better future for everyone.

I suggest the opposite is true. The exchange mentality in fact creates poverty, enforces disparity, fosters social injustice, causes conflict and undermines our hopes for a sustainable future in which there is "enough, for all, forever."

Because the exchange mentality is at the heart of our global economic system, we need to change the game, not just some of the players or what they do. Solutions embedded in the exchange economy will only maintain the very structures that created the problem.

Any exchange is based upon inequality. Someone else has what you want or need. The hope is that you also have something they want or need, so that the exchange is possible and both parties leave with more than they arrived and are satisfied by the transaction. The problems start when the inequality does not end with the transaction. Perhaps one side has nothing present to exchange, so the offer is made of some future compensation or exchange (such as the interest on a loan). Perhaps one side only gets a portion of what they want or need, because they lack what is necessary to even up their side of the exchange.

Exchange creates poverty. Poverty is not simply *being* poor, it is *feeling* poor. Poverty is the consequence of comparison between your condition and that of someone else, realizing that they have something you do not. Exchange between unequal parties means one party has nothing to give back. Out of inequality and disparity comes despair – because no matter what the medium of currency or exchange, the weaker party will never catch up.

In an exchange mentality, the powerful may befriend the weak, just as the wealthy may befriend the poor. Yet the weaker party may find it hard to accept that they have equal status. Out of that imbalance comes suspicion ("what do they really want from me?"), resentment ("I am always the poor cousin") and jealousy ("I wish I could control my life the same way"). These feelings, even between friends, arouse the potential for alienation and conflict.

In the larger society, those possibilities for suspicion, resentment and conflict multiply exponentially. Even efforts to promote social justice falter or fail, not because of the things that are done, but because of the cultural system within which they are done. When there is no such thing as a free lunch, even apparent generosity must have a catch or hidden cost.

The debate about sustainable development is good example of the values inherent in the exchange economy. Countries in the North concerned about sustainability argue for the need to exclude development from the equation – there is already too much development, which is why the planet is in trouble. Countries in the South, whose standard of living lags behind that of the North, argue that development is crucial to providing the basic necessities of life for their people. Without that development, the South will never match the North; yet, given the global set of economic and political rules that keep the playing field unequal, they will not catch up before the planet implodes for any number of reasons.

This is at heart a problem with how economics has been misconstrued since the eighteenth century. "Economics" is from the Greek *oikonomia,* meaning care for the household, or the equivalent idea of stewardship: one's responsibility was to care for one's inheritance from the past generation (in the form of land and its attachments) and pass it along improved to the next. Economics is no longer about *oikonomia* – it is about metrics. We now have indices of quality of life, as well as happiness, easily linked to Gross Domestic Product (GDP), Gross National Product (GNP) and whatever else we choose to number and count. If we can count it, we can measure it; if we can measure it, we can exchange it.

At the end of his Gifford Lectures, published as *The Nature of the Physical World* (1928), astronomer Arthur Eddington mused that we all live in two universes, the metrical and the non-metrical – the universe of things that can be counted and measured and the universe of things that cannot. Surprising his audience, Eddington in effect concluded that everything of value was to be found in the non-metrical universe. His observation goes straight to the heart of the problem we face today. A sustainable future requires a radical shift in metrics – a shift in every sense, from population to climate change to all the other numbers that indicate the growing fury of Gaia. Those metrics are grounded in an exchange economy that cannot comprehend the reality that what is offered, on all sides, must be valued rather than measured.

The answer to the problem, I argue, is to be found in the significance of a gift.

The argument itself is simple: The attitudes and values associated with the economics of exchange are in large part to blame for our current unsustainable situation. We need to rediscover what it means to live in a universe of relations, not merely on a planet that can be counted, measured and used. The more we are able to replace an economy based on transactions with an ecology based on gifts, the more likely a sustainable future becomes for all of Earth's children.

Without "gift ecology," our individual efforts – no matter how Herculean – toward creating social, cultural, economic or environmental sustainability will be unsuccessful.

These conclusions will require more than the rest of this book to unpack and explain. What follows is an outline of ideas, opportunities for further thought and reflection, all in an effort to reimagine the sustainable world that could result from the radical social and cultural transformation "gift ecology" requires.

It is written for you – literally. Whatever fictions might be advanced about authors and their readers, I believe a book is a highly personal encounter. It is as personal as where you are at the very moment you read this sentence. It is as personal as what you have chosen not to do because, instead, you are reading what I have written. It is subjective, because what you think after reading this book will not be the same as what someone else has thought, nor will your emotions and conclusions match someone else's except by coincidence or caricature.

So – person to person, and all contrivances of authorship and readership aside – I want to make you think. I want to make you think about where we are right now; about what makes our culture and our society unsustainable; about what is really going on in material terms with our planet, beyond the parameters of politics or academic dispute. I want you to consider what is possible to change immediately and what will be more difficult – though just as necessary – to change in the near future.

Individual empowerment is about thinking first, not just acting. As in the old carpenter's maxim, we need to measure twice and saw once. But it is not about being paralyzed by the need to gather "all the facts" first, by requiring indisputable metrics before finally choosing to do something. The Earth's system is dynamic, as are the human systems with which it engages. Therefore we will never have a perfect time to act. All we have is the moment. We can see only dimly into whatever possibilities the future holds. That dim future merely shades our choices in a particular direction, however – it does not determine them. Nor does what we choose necessarily result in what we think is going to happen.

Reimagining a sustainable world requires us to navigate between two realities, as between Scylla and Charybdis, neither wrecked upon the rock of despair nor sucked into the whirlpool of helplessness.

ə❧

There are two main parts to the book, with an interlude between them. In the first part, we look at three characteristics of industrial society and culture and discuss their relationship to the predominance of the exchange economy.

In the second part, we reflect on the difference between what is given and what is Gift. The alternative to the exchange economy– gift ecology within a universe of relations – is presented and its implications for sustainability explained.

As prelude, we begin with a brief depiction of the technology that underpins both our unsustainable present and our hopes for a sustainable future.

ॐ

Prelude

On Ethics, Technology and Sustainability

Technology is in our heads, not in our hands. We live in a world of our own choosing.

Everything about technology starts with a choice. It is sometimes hard to see this. Every day, we are constrained by technology, forced into lock-step as we log into our daily routines. We have choices – we are just not encouraged by mass culture to see them for what they are.

Ask a group of people whether they have made an ethical choice so far today, and most will say "no." Yet each us of makes hundreds of such choices, every day – from what we wear, to how we travel, to what we eat, to how we behave. If we do not recognize these choices for what they are, we are still making them. We are just not thinking about them first.

If you want an explanation for the

unsustainable condition of our planet, this would be half of it. We make decisions without thinking about what we are doing. Even if today we make brilliantly sustainable ethical choices, we can have no expectation that we will do the same thing tomorrow. Nor should we – after all, we did not realize what we were deciding today! This explains why perfectly intelligent, reasonable and well-intentioned people can consistently make foolish and dangerous decisions. Quite literally, they were not thinking clearly enough about what they were choosing – or perhaps not thinking at all.

We need to think about what we are choosing, all the time, each of us, every day. When we consider the implications for ourselves, for other people and for our planet, it leads to a much more intentional life – and likely to a shift in the choices we make.

But this leads to the other half of the explanation. We are not only making choices without thinking. We are making them about something we don't understand – technology. This may sound crazy, as we are all citizens of a global technological society, but it is true. If you were to ask the average person "What is technology?" you would get a certain range of answers: technology is recent, if not new; it is mechanical and certainly electrical; it involves devices and gadgets; it's what we use to make our lives easier, to develop the human race toward some brighter future, reflected in growth and optimism about progress.

We are indoctrinated with the idea that Western technology (and the science that co-exists with it) is better than anything else from anywhere else, whether in terms of chronology or geography. New is better than old. Urban and Western is better than rural and southern. If any of these thoughts reflect your own definition of technology, consider the following: Technology is not new. It goes back to when Grok picked up the rock for the first time and threw it at a sabre-toothed tiger. Technology has been with us since the dawn of human culture. It is what makes us human. Every culture, every society, therefore, has had its own technology. It was not the same as ours, obviously, but it was what they needed to survive.

Getting rid of the emotional blackmail

associated with "progress," therefore, is a first step toward reimagining a sustainable world. Instead of being for or against progress, we must focus on which technology is appropriate for doing what we need to do. Whether it is new or old, appropriate technology is whatever works. Appropriate technology should also mean sustainable technology, technology that – at the very least – does no harm.

This leads back to where we started – technology is in our heads, not in our hands. It does not exist apart from the decisions made to create or to use it. Technology is *never* neutral. It is always the product of choices; choices are for reasons; and those reasons reflect the values of the people doing the choosing.

We can do some reverse engineering of the values embedded in our technology. We can work back from an object of technology to the choices that led to its creation and use. From there, we can figure out why it was developed and what values lay behind those reasons. If we don't like the values we realize are reflected in our technology, we can change them – and that then changes the definition of appropriate technology.

Technology is never isolated, either: it exists in systems. If we want to understand technology, we also have to understand the complex of social, cultural and environmental systems related to it. Together, all these systems embed values. If you really want to change outcomes, the starting point is the value set, what people as individuals (and in larger groups, as societies and cultures) think is important.

So the choice is ours alone. Technology is instrumental knowledge and its practice, knowledge that we use to do something, for reasons that reflect the values we think are important. It is practical knowledge, appropriate to the circumstances in which we find ourselves, responsive to the problems and concerns of the here and now.

Because technology is in our heads, individuals and societies that make the right choices survive. Those that make the wrong choices do not. Look back in history, and you will find examples of right and wrong choices and their outcomes.

Our society is no different than any other in history, and as individuals we are not immune from the consequences of bad choices about technology. It may be frightening to think that so much rides on what we choose, but in this there is both hope and good news:

First, we have choices, just as other people have always had. Nothing is foreordained or determined when it comes to technology. Technology is neither neutral nor autonomous, with a mind of its own. We decide, still.

Second, we have far more tools and uses for them than we realize – because the most important one is between our ears. We just need to think more clearly about what kind of technology is appropriate, regardless of whether it is new or old, complex or simple. Technology will shape our future, as it has always done – but it is our choice what tools to use and to what end.

Finally, choice is about empowerment and responsibility – for all of us. Everyone makes choices. Everyone should think about what they are choosing and why, and ask what values are reflected in their choices.

Every time we think for ourselves and make a choice (however small) toward a sustainable future, the universe shifts. Mass culture would tell us of the futility of our individual choices and actions, but from the perspectives of history and experience, this is simply not true. We still choose the future. We just need to think more clearly about the choices we are making toward it, every day, if we want to reimagine what it means to live in a sustainable world.

PART 1

*Mechanics,
Methodists
and Me*

1. The Mechanical "I"

To understand technology from the perspective of the Old Savage, we need to get inside his head, to realize what lay behind the choices that early humans made about the technology that came to define civilization.

Early technology addressed human vulnerability. Tools were identified, developed and used to extend the strength and reach of our physical abilities. We could not outrun the animals we needed for food, so we developed weapons to kill them from a distance. Vulnerable to the teeth and claws of other carnivores, we developed more effective and lethal mechanical ones. Vulnerable to the elements, we found ways to clothe ourselves, to use and then to create fire, to build or find shelter from the weather. Vulnerable to the risks of hunting and gathering through constant migration, we settled in one area and developed the resources to sustain ourselves through agriculture and the domestication of animals.

All of these vulnerabilities drive the basic technologies of any civilization, including our own. What changed about five hundred years ago was that Europeans came to conceive of their own physical identity in terms of mechanisms. Specifically, the metaphor of the machine had its earliest and most successful philosophical application to the human body in the period of the Renaissance. Whether or not the rise of humanism reflected the idea that Man was "the measure of all things," the mechanical metaphor certainly meant that men and women should be measured.

One of the fascinating things about the Renaissance is the "discovery" of perspective and how it related to the detailed drawings, paintings and sculptures that depicted the human body in such a realistic way. Associated with the anatomical detail, of course, was anatomical dissection – something akin to a boxing match today, as spectators thronged the galleries to watch anatomists pull out and display cadaver parts, ostensibly in the interests of medical education.

The other side of this macabre interest, however, was the desire to mimic or replicate the mechanical motions of the body. Underneath the skin was something anatomists now recognized as a mechanism; they figured out how bones and muscles worked together to create the mechanics of movement. Illustrations in surgical texts included cutaway drawings of parts, like the hand, where the movements were associated with different cogs and levers. It is no surprise, therefore, that the keenest interest in human anatomy and structure was associated with one of the great engineering minds of the Renaissance. Leonardo da Vinci saw in the body and the machine parallels to be exploited.

The self-conscious representation of human anatomy and physiology as mechanism, the mechanical "I," marked the beginning of the mechanical metaphor, which reached its high-water mark by the late nineteenth century. Understanding the movements of the body through its anatomy led to the perception that all systems, including organic ones, could be represented and reproduced as mechanisms behaving in linear, causally related sequences.

Classification of organisms through the association of their physical features took place at the same time as diseases began to be classified by their symptoms and etiology. The model for this was physics and astronomy, in which the motions of the heavenly bodies were recognized as an extension of motions that could be replicated on earth. The universe itself was a giant mechanism, perhaps started by a Deity but needing no further intervention – the mechanism itself had taken over and developed in a predictable fashion from that point onward.

Electricity was the last leap: it became identified as the animating force that separated living matter from dead. But mechanisms are not organisms. If we forget that fact, like Mary Shelley's Dr. Frankenstein, we risk creating a monster that threatens to destroy more than its creator. The nineteenth-century Romantic backlash against mechanism, the push for something more and other, reflected the age-old human experience of self and the natural world.

The trajectory of our current problem, therefore, extends back at least five hundred years. There is a fundamental flaw in understanding the universe as a mechanism, whether it is one that unfolds mathematically from the Big Bang to the present or one in which organisms are explained in a linear and connected fashion. The basic truth – that life is not mechanical and that organisms are not machines – seems not to be understood.

The Mechanic (or Mechanician) appears in many guises in our society, the most obvious of which is as a technician or an engineer, but the mechanical attitude itself has become embedded in all aspects of our conception of the world and in the way we relate to it and to each other. We talk about connections, not relations, as though the universe and everything in it was part of some giant Meccano set that we could build and rebuild if we only had the right pieces. The mechanical metaphor and its associated vocabulary dwarf any other representation of life, creating too simplistic an understanding of natural systems and presuming an ability to understand and manipulate natural systems to suit human objectives.

If we want to understand an elephant, it seems we begin by slicing and dicing it into its component pieces. While we learn much about its structure and anatomy, we can never reassemble the pieces into a real elephant. We also learn little about what it means to be an elephant, or to be part of system that includes elephants, when we use such methods.

If we want to understand the physical universe, we look for ultimate particles; we build bigger and bigger machines to smash things smaller and smaller, to the point that the only limit on how small we can go is how big a machine we can build.

Nor do advances in biology change this predisposition to the mechanical and the connected. In the 1920s, physicists had essentially dismissed the traditional idea of a material universe, but with the discovery of the "building blocks of life" (DNA) in the 1950s, biologists and geneticists nonchalantly reintroduced it as an explanation for inheritance and thus for every living thing.

Nowhere else perhaps is this mechanical attitude toward the human body, the assertion of the mechanical "I," more apparent than in the practice of Western biomedicine. The successes that have followed from thinking about the body-as-mechanism are extraordinary. When body parts wear out or break, we manufacture increasingly sophisticated replacements; now that we also understand other forms of life in mechanical terms, we can even get replacements from non-human donors.

The biomedical system is much less able to understand the art of healing, however, than it is able to research, fund and implement the practice of fixing. Reduce mental illness to biochemical malfunction, and we can add the missing chemicals. Learn the genetic dimensions of congenital abnormalities, and we hold out the possibility of fixing those humans who do not measure up to some ostensible norm of human health and development. Consider disease to be an enemy, and the immune system takes on a military cast that requires us to boost the body's defences or commandeer them to fight some pathogenic invasion.

Biomedicine has the least success addressing problems involving interrelated systems, not because of a lack of tools, but because the mechanical "I" does not easily accept holistic explanations. Our bodies are not isolated from our environment, nor is "human" necessarily distinct from the range of micro-organisms inside and outside the skin that make our life possible. If the immune system is perceived as a muscle needing exercise, this leads to different strategies for health than if the body is seen as a medieval castle needing to repel invaders intent on its destruction.

Similarly, without understanding the weave of environmental, social and cultural factors involved, we cannot reduce mental health to rebalancing chemicals in the brain. The homeless people with psychiatric issues whose numbers have multiplied on the streets of the urban West are coincidental with the mechanical view of mental illness that, as a society, we have so crudely applied.

What society thinks makes us human is in effect what society comes to value as being human, which is why efforts to "fix" physical and mental abnormalities have disturbing implications for how people with disabilities are viewed. Is someone with one arm of less value than someone with two? Is a child with an IQ of 180 twice as valuable as one with an IQ of 90 – perhaps with twice the right to life and social opportunity?

Understanding the body as a machine, promoting the concept of the mechanical "I," leads inevitably to the metrical valuation of what it means to be human. Whether the numbers are physical measures or measures of ability – or both – value has been reduced to an arbitrary standard against which people's lives are measured in isolation from the social, cultural and environmental systems within which we are all interrelated.

After all, everything relates; only some things connect. We live in a universe of relations, not the environment of connections that the mechanical "I" assumes. When we focus only on connections, we leave ourselves only poor, linear tools to analyze systems that are inherently nonlinear. We try to understand system complexity in terms of linear causality, looking for causal connections that will never be found, reducing Nature to a bucket of bolts. We assume the role of Her mechanic, changing, connecting, fixing, recreating and (dare we say it?) improving what we find to better suit our own wisdom and purposes. Whether or not people believe in God, there is certainly plenty of evidence that people like to play God when it comes to making irreversible changes to the Earth.

Any such interventionist role implies control over Nature. Perhaps our fixation with the mechanical "I" is the result of the psychological vulnerability of the Old Savage, who by himself was never fast enough or strong enough to withstand the perils his environment presented. Technology has served from the beginning to control our environment, to shape the world around us, to provide shelter from the elements that made our ancestors huddle together in fear. We have been hugely successful over time, and so when nature intervenes to remind us of our place in the Earth story, it often takes a catastrophe to get our attention. Hurricanes, earthquakes, tornados, tsunamis, typhoons – these demonstrate the force with which our defences and our very civilization can be hammered and even destroyed by the power that lurks in Nature.

Humans have a short attention span. Our eyes (and our mind's eye in particular) focus on the close at hand, the immediate, the latest bauble that happens to glitter by. Increasingly since the Renaissance of the 15th century, we have mistaken force for power, and have substituted our knowledge of the mechanisms we can manipulate for wisdom as to how we should live with each other and with the Earth.

Have a conversation about the power of Nature, and you will not hear much talk of butterflies and earthworms. Yet Nature's power has nothing to do with what we understand to be force. We merely don't see it and so we remain dissociated, despite our best efforts, from the essence of the life change going on all around us. The earth actually moves under our feet every day; it just takes an earthquake to get our attention. Anytime we stop to actually look at the earth, it is overwhelming – on a small scale – beyond anything we could even attempt to mimic with our own models and constructions.

The evidence has always been there for those with the wisdom and the eyes to see it. There has been a split since the early days of the mythical Scientific Revolution, when human eyes were turned to the heavens, the movements of which became the subject of telescopic investigations and mathematical calculations – and inspired the discovery of physical laws of motion in nature.

So the roll of heroes includes Galileo, Kepler, Newton, Copernicus and others of their ilk. As physics and chemistry developed, the discovery of simple reactions and physical interactions led to changes in everything from metallurgy to manufacturing – all arguably extensions of the mechanical outlook into the physical world.

But simultaneous with the discovery of power, whether in the form of water, coal or steam, other players were in the wings; their initial discoveries were made at the same time as the telescope revealed the heavens. Antonij van Leeuwenhoek invented the microscope at much the same time as Galileo turned his telescope to the heavens. Robert Boyle delighted his seventeenth-century audience at the Royal Society with his mechanisms, just as its curator of experiments, Robert Hooke, published *Micrographia*, with its pictures of a world, invisible to the eye, that the microscope allowed us to explore.

Physics and chemistry dealt in atomism and mechanism, the laws of physical nature, the mechanical mimicry of natural motions. Motions and trajectories could be calculated and predicted, giving tangible evidence of how well we understood how the universe worked. Science dealing with life, however, still faced the mystery of what made something alive – a problem no amount of anatomical dissection could solve. Organisms could be observed from the outside but not explained. Then came the discovery of electricity, followed closely by electromagnetic theory, and the secret that tied life to matter seemed to be solved, at least in the popular imagination

So, against the power of Nature, we asserted our own power. We have changed the planet by design, using its material resources at the whim of our inexhaustible need, and have lost sight of where the real power lies. Yet we should never underestimate a butterfly, nor disregard an earthworm.

We live in relation with all the elements of the Earth system, related in ways more subtle than we can begin to imagine. Whatever we can say about the relations among people, just consider the ways in which humans relate to animals – cats, dogs and other pets – and how that rapport shapes people's lives. Imagine what that would mean if it were consciously extended to other creatures and to the planet itself. If we had the capacity to see down to the smallest of all things, to see into the centre of the web of life, then we would understand why and how all the universe relates, but we don't.

Where we do damage, and where the struggle for sustainability ultimately will take place, is in the majority of the biosphere we cannot see. We need to reassert the balance that has been lost – but even now, when we can see some of the complexities of living systems, we lack the tools to manage them. But if technology is in our heads rather than in our hands, then the problem is not in our tools but in ourselves. We need to look for different ways of understanding both the problem and its solution.

At the heart of any solution must first be a change in the language we use. Words matter, especially if we want to reimagine a sustainable world. Words have the power both to open new possibilities and to set horizons to what we are able to see.

We need to integrate what humans have learned over thousands of years into a new synthesis with what science and technology have

learned about the universe and how it works –
and to show some judgment and humility in the
process.

It is arrogance that leads us to assume we can
fix anything that breaks and that we need to
swing away at whatever obstacle we encounter.
In discussions about sustainability, we auto-
matically talk about environmental "impact,"
assuming in all our relations with Nature the
necessity of a hammer's force. Even the environmental "footprint," as powerful a symbol as
it is for depicting our exploitation of the planet,
substitutes a crude concept of interference for
an understanding of the weave of all life. How
does it affect our relations with the earth if we
can only conceive of them in negative terms of
minimizing our impact, instead of seeing the
positive interrelationships we have with all elements of the Earth system?

A second issue is therefore that of separation.
We are not separate from the Earth, nor are
the buildings we construct. Such separation is
illusory. Put two people in a room together and
we can calculate mathematically how long it will
take for atoms from the innermost part of one

person to travel to the innermost parts of the other. There can be no more intimate relation than this – but we pretend it does not happen. At a microscopic level, we cannot live without the micro-organisms that literally recreate us from the inside out, every day. Yet when we believe the wrong ones have taken control, we use antibiotic weapons of mass destruction to wipe out everything within range.

New values and new possibilities emerge from viewing our bodies in terms of relation, not separation, from the Earth. Natural systems include us, shaping our lives with the same power that enables a trickle of water to change a mountain over the course of time. We need to align ourselves and what we do with the power of Nature, not merely contend against its force.

We need to understand sustainability in ways that include all life on (and in) the planet, not just our own. But there are no computer systems able to replicate the complexity of the web of life, nor will we ever create mechanisms as tools that would enable us to manage that complexity. Our wisdom needs to respect the butterfly and appreciate the earthworm — and not mistake their lack of force as evidence of their lack of power.

That wisdom, to find the power in subtleties, to live with the Earth and not against it, resonates with many dimensions of our cultural heritage that the metrics of industrial economies have tended to ignore. It also runs counter to the methodical extension of the mechanical "I" into every aspect of our understanding of the universe and of how we live in it.

ॐ

2. The Methodical Muse

If the Old Savage's response to his vulnerabilities was to create and use the tools he needed – first to protect himself and then to change his environment to provide more dependable long-term protection – then repetition was important. It wasn't enough for something to work once; it had to work every time. Repetition, consistency, dependability – all these qualities are extensions of the desire for technology to do the same things today and tomorrow as it did yesterday.

This desire led to systems sufficiently simple that their causal mechanisms could be understood in linear terms. One thing leads to another, every time. If you do that, this is what happens, every time. Even complex systems could be understood in these terms, as long as they could be broken down into sub-systems that each functioned in an equivalent way, every time.

The complexity of traditional local knowledge, however, reflects trial and error over many generations. It might take an apprentice a lifetime to acquire the knowledge and skills of a master craftsman, or years of experience to understand how to manage crops and livestock to produce food without fail and enable the community's survival.

As the idea of the mechanical "I" was extended into mechanical systems, the complexities of traditional knowledge were replaced by much simpler processes based upon a particular function. The simpler the process, the better it was, because it could be repeated more easily and had a more predictable outcome.

In her Massey Lectures, published in 1989 as *The Real World of Technology*, Ursula Franklin distinguished between two types of technological systems, holistic and prescriptive, pointing out that while both have existed for a very long time, holistic systems have everywhere been replaced by prescriptive ones since the first Industrial Revolution (c. 1750).

In holistic technology, one person is identifiably in charge of the whole process of producing an item – making decisions about everything from the design to the materials, to how it is made and when it is finished. This is the "craft" process, something best illustrated in the activities of a potter creating a bowl of his or her own design.

In prescriptive technology, the production process is broken down into a series of steps. Each step is assigned to a different person, requiring them to comply with the overall pattern set down and overseen by a manager. Whereas in the holistic model a craftsman has control over the whole process, individual difference is not permitted in the prescriptive model by the process itself or by the manager in charge of it. By another name, prescriptive technology is the factory system, what is at the core of any mass production process. Franklin's point, however, is that such systems have existed for a very long time. Only recently have they come to dominate not only how we make things but also how we see ourselves and our world.

The success of the mechanical "I" led to the desire for its extension into other areas. The consequence was not only the factory system, but the inspiration of "the methodical Muse" in all aspects of Western industrial culture. Our unsustainable society therefore reflects not only a fixation on the mechanical view of the body, but also its extension through method to a mechanical view of how we should live together in the world.

Reimagining a sustainable world requires us not only to counter the physical isolation of the mechanical 'I' but also the methodical extension that leads us to conceive of all systems in mechanical terms. It requires us to challenge that most cherished of modern mythologies, the scientific method, which supposedly emerged at the same time as the mechanical metaphor seized the Western cultural imagination.

While the scientific method is the root myth of modern Western culture, it never actually existed. To call something a myth is not to say it is false, but to say it has the same cultural role as other myths. Whether it is the anger of Zeus, the heroism of Hercules, the hammer of Thor or the trickery of Loki, mythology continues to frame the story of who we are in relation to the meaning of the universe. Every culture has its own mythology, the stories that are passed down from generation to generation, and these myths or stories create the foundation on which our world is built.

To call the scientific method a myth, therefore, is not to say it has no power to shape our view of the universe. It merely never existed as something that could be kicked, something solid and identifiable not only in theory but in its historical operation. People believe it exists, so (as a myth) it does. People believe they are following it when they do what they understand to be "science," so the myth of the scientific method continues to influence our view of the universe.

The confusion arises from the belief that scientists use the scientific method to discover truths about that universe. Historians, philosophers and social scientists – particularly sociologists – have studied many facets of the activities of science over the past five hundred years since the Scientific Revolution (an event that Steven Shapin, in his book by the same name, also observed didn't exist). Whatever similarities there are from circumstance to circumstance, to extrapolate some overarching "scientific method" is only possible by doing violence to the evidence.

Western culture since the seventeenth century demonstrates the importance not of one particular method, but of Method in general. It is more accurate and more useful to consider how the concept of Method became a Muse for every facet of the industrial culture that emerged from the Renaissance. The scientific method is but one myth among a number of similar ones about Method, even if it is the most prominently portrayed.

We need to think in terms of the "methodical Muse," not the scientific method, if we want to understand the social and cultural parameters of the industrial culture that, in its turn, has led to our unsustainable present. The Muse itself emerges from the mechanical world view, leading "method" to be understood only in mechanical, repetitive and predictable terms that reflect both materiality and linear causality.

Beginning with simple, repetitive systems and motions – which is why it was more about mechanics than organics – methodical investigation led generally to discoveries in the mechanics of how the world goes together. Increasingly those depictions were mathematical, the systems linear, logical and predictable in their causal relations.

Ropes, pulleys, cogs, wheels, springs and other mechanical devices – these were the stuff of Industrial Revolution. Add the discoveries in chemistry and metallurgy that heralded the industrial societies of nineteenth-century Europe, along with the motive powers of steam and electricity, and the Age of Power was present in all of its forceful manifestations.

Systems had parts, were causally connected and functioned according to a discernible, linear logic. Efforts to replicate natural systems by mechanical means dated at least to the Renaissance (witness the drawings of da Vinci, if not also his medieval or even Roman predecessors, like Vitruvius); their social extension reflected the application of similar principles to society in general and to human interactions in particular.

John Wesley's Methodists were derided in the eighteenth century for their schedules of religious observances, but routine and regularity, method and prescription, were shown to have other benefits in the development and organization of society, from factories to how people lived together. Method became the rage. So much of the European industrial culture that developed from the seventeenth through the twentieth centuries was inspired by the methodical Muse that even the concept of ecology itself may can be traced to a Romantic reaction to the development of economic thinking, with its metaphors of mechanical systems, that was a product of the late eighteenth century.

Whether or not might made right, it certainly made good economic sense. European countries moved to expand and solidify their holdings in other parts of the world where resources were readily available and markets for goods easily established. The systems of wartime economies, themselves a product of the Napoleonic period, were manifested in everything from the logistics of moving armies, to the mechanics of sailing ships, to the functions of imperial colonial trade around the globe.

Method was increasingly applied to operations of finance and economics, and while the instruments available at the time did not match the earliest theories of how economies should function, the potential for economic control – and its desirability, as a way of managing the whims of the masses – was argued on all sides. Whether one was a Marxist or a laissez-faire capitalist, a libertarian or a socialist, the presumption on all sides favoured method, organization and social control – just according to differing principles and varying views on whether those principles were part of the "natural order" or required human assertion.

Everywhere, money accrued to method, and power was methodically developed and extended. Mechanical means enabled the military to succeed where diplomacy could not. If, for example, there was any doubt about the value of a General Staff system in organizing and conducting a war, it quickly vanished with the smoke of the Prussian victory over France in 1870–71. Similarly, whatever the actual value of the use of railroads in that war, their symbolic value was apparent – make the trains run on time, with the right stuff, to the right place, and military as well as economic advantage was guaranteed.

This kind of method was narrowly construed, however, more a reflection of mechanical than philosophical principles and their application to accomplishing a specific task. Efficiency was measured in terms of how to move so many boxes from Point A to Point B in the fastest time with the least effort and at the lowest cost. It was the industrial-scale application of practical, goal-oriented thinking, not some larger view of the universe reflected in the mythology of the scientific method.

Science before the nineteenth century depended entirely on the generosity of patrons with the money to spend on what amounted to little more than whim. Characterized more accurately as "natural philosophy," it can be equated to modern science only by ignoring the evidence, such as the fact that Isaac Newton wrote more theology than physics and was more interested in alchemy than mathematics. Even in the nineteenth century, the scientific method existed more in popular imagination than it ever did in the practice of science. Historians and sociologists of science have demonstrated this repeatedly, to the dismay of non-practitioners with a romantic view of the profession and its efforts toward objectivity and detachment.

What came to be understood as "science" was fuelled by desire for the money and fame associated with the prizes set by individuals, industries and governments; the case of Louis Pasteur was perhaps the most blatant. What was methodical was the way in which social and industrial problems were addressed and solved, with patents secured for future earnings on the solutions that industry required right away. Thomas Edison's Menlo Park facility became a model for how successful scientific research should be methodically undertaken – success was measured by the numbers of patents and their earnings, not some more noble philosophical goal.

As this methodical development was taking place in science, the desire for increased and more profitable production led first to the factory system and then to mass production. Industry wanted to replace labour with machinery, even if the machines had not yet made this goal practical. The canal system in Great Britain was supplanted and then replaced by the railroad, even though it took decades (and the bankruptcy of many personal fortunes) before it could carry the freight needed to support an industrial economy that the canal system was already able to handle.

Since one of the characteristics of a mechanical system is the ability to repeat a process and get an expected and desired result, success bred imitation. This kind of predictability attracted investors. Whether real or illusory, predictability meant control. The methodical Muse implied to her followers the predictable benefits of power, wealth and control. These proved so irresistible to so many that evidence of the darker side of the application of mechanical systems to natural or human systems was ignored.

Knowledge was Power, everywhere in evidence from the steam engine to the marvels that industrial society was able to accomplish. The Crystal Palace Exhibition of 1851 and the various exhibitions held elsewhere through to the Great War demonstrated the triumphs of mechanism and method over the obstacles to survival that Nature had presented to the Old Savage since the beginning of time itself.

The reverse was also assumed, that somehow that Power was Knowledge – what could or needed to be known was determined by those whose role in the new mechanical society justified such expertise. If there was one heroic professional in the industrial age, it became the Engineer, whose knowledge of mechanical principles was translated into the mastery of Nature by his minions and whose ingenious machinery was tended by clever mechanics.

Nature was represented as a physical problem to be addressed, solved, scaled and conquered, from crossing the oceans to reach the North and South Pole, to exploring the heart of Africa and the source of the Amazon, to climbing Mount Everest. Add internal combustion to the picture, and speed, altitude and distance became barriers to shatter on land, at sea and in the air.

The absence of wisdom from both of these equations lies at the heart of the misuse of industrial machinery that has brought us to our unsustainable present. The measurement of Knowledge and Power in financial terms led straight to the dominance of the exchange economy over other means of understanding society, culture and human relations with the Earth.

The industrial method always treated people as means to an end, fuel for the Machine, fodder for some voracious Beast. As depicted before the Great War of 1914–18 in the gloom of Charles Dickens's novels, and afterward in the bleak vision of Fritz Lang's *Metropolis* and the social satire of Charlie Chaplin's *Modern Times,* the New Civilization had its dark side.

The question was asked again and again: what had been lost in the process of conquering Nature? What was missing from the New Civilization, for all its glitter and accomplishments? What had taken Western society into the maelstrom of industrial-scale warfare and the rapid devastation of empires?

When the Great War was followed by the Crash of 1929 and the collapse of the global economy into the Great Depression, there was a lot of popular rumination on the future of Western civilization. In the 1920s and 1930s, Raymond Fosdick was not alone in his concerns about the kind of moral developments that were needed if the Old Savage was going to have much of a future in the New Civilization.

It was, however, the Age of Isms. The siren song of the methodical Muse lured various countries to intensify their efforts to create the kind of civilization that the methodical application of certain philosophical principles entailed. Whether it was fascism in Germany and Italy (and also in Japan, one might argue), New Deal capitalism in the United States, or state socialism in the Soviet Union, each involved aligning all elements of society toward a common goal through a common orientation and method. It led – again – to war, in 1939.

In the aftermath of World War II, the supposed Cold War split between Western capitalism and Soviet or Chinese communism was more illusion than reality. In fact, both operated according to essentially the same method. Communism may have vigorously dissuaded the practice of religion, but the values inherent in post-War capitalism arguably made religion equally irrelevant in practical terms to what people did and how they viewed themselves and their world.

On all sides, the real deity (with apologies to John Wesley) was Methodism. Value was attached not to originality or individuality, but to compliance with the prescriptive requirements of the mechanistic system. As postwar Western industrial society became more integrated and interconnected, personal compliance became just as dominant a virtue in the West as it was under state socialism or communism in the East. Even before computers brought us into the Age of Log-In, compliance and obedience were valued more highly than individuality and rebellion – and were financially rewarded.

Efficiency of all kinds came to be measured in economic terms and was rewarded with increased productivity and profits. The Cold War economic and political duel between East and West might have been won by the West, but the terms of the fight and its outcomes were decided by the methodical Muse, who inspired all sides according to the same mechanical principles.

To be clear, there is nothing wrong with Method. It is how we apply what we know to how we live; it is how we shape who we are and what we do. But there are many different ways of being methodical, depending on our understanding of the principles involved. When these are applied to organic systems, they are not necessarily as linear, neat and predictable as a Mechanist would prefer.

It is the combination of Mechanism and

Methodism that leads to the representation of human beings in mechanical and methodical terms, as components of constructed systems within which they are placed to live and work. To reimagine a sustainable world, our method needs to reflect principles other than mechanical ones, and our personal identities need to be valued rather than measured. Otherwise, we are left only with the externalities of "the metrical Me."

3. The Metrical "Me"

It is ironic that René Descartes's *cogito ergo sum* ("I think, therefore I am") in *Discourse on Method* (1637) led to "the metrics of me." Descartes divided the world into things that think and things that don't – thinking matter and extended matter. In a world of objects, therefore, each thinking person has an identity that is separate, distinct and unique.

It was an idea that caught on. Personal identity became something derived not from social relation but from self-conception. Like James Boswell in his *London Journal* of 1762–63 we can assume whatever guise or role we choose. There is a direct line from Descartes's assertion to the explosion of English autobiographical literature that took place in the eighteenth century. Since then, think of how many memoirs have been published, autobiographies not only of the rich and famous but of the uninteresting and unimportant. Then reflect on the presumption of the twenty-first-century tweeter and blogger that someone "out there" cares about anything an individual thinks, regardless of whether it is serious or inane.

Self-identity, like self-worth, has become something we can count and measure, like our weight or the number of shoes in our closet. We are defined by who and what we are, as opposed to the system within which we are placed or found. Individuation has led to the metrics of self. Identity becomes defined metrically, effectively in isolation from any social context except those that we decide are important.

So what matters is the number of Facebook friends we have, or followers on Twitter, not who they are or what they might mean to us or to anyone else. It is the numbers we can generate – sales figures, dollars earned, achievements counted, benchmarks reached, goals accomplished, records set – that matters, not who we are. In some circles, where you went to school matters more than what you studied or anything that you learned.

Meet someone new at a party, and the first question beyond the exchange of names is "what do you do?" Someone without a job and the metrics that it brings – such as income – lacks a social and cultural identity and is not only embarrassed but is embarrassing to be around. Jobs bring with them their own social pecking order – better to be a secretary than a plumber, even though being a plumber may require more skills and plumbing is a more lucrative profession. Better to be an executive with authority and stock options than a secretary, even though it is the secretary that actually makes the organization function. Academic credentials bring instant social recognition, even if the Ph.D. serves no purpose more useful than covering a hole in the office wall.

From the early days of the Industrial Revolution, social status was increasingly measured not by social rank but by economic condition – with the second readily agreed to be an acceptable means of acquiring the first. Whether or not knowledge was power, it certainly meant money, and money was the means to acquire power. The grubby (but wealthy) captains of industry married off their daughters to the (penniless) sons of privilege to forever mix social distinction with industrial prowess.

We are defined as separate and definite entities, not in terms of our relations with other people or with the planet. Numbers serve to reinforce this individual and personal identity. Anthropocentrism is the natural result of such a perspective, because Man quite literally is the measure of all things. Material reality dominates, because it is all we can see and kick, and that material reality starts with our own metrical identity.

Everything is done by the numbers. The government uses numbers for social identification – for purposes not only of taxation but also of social security, allowing us to drive a car or be subject to compulsory military service. Value and opportunity are everywhere defined numerically and usually represented in material and financial terms.

The consequence of this metrical identity is the increase in consumption that has marked Western industrial society and its inheritors. Growth is represented as perpetual – something actually not possible in an organic system – and linear, measured in terms of what can be sliced, diced and counted. Everything is seen as a potential input for the Machine. Resources are there to be used and consumed, Nature exists as a source of raw material, and we are the means by which things are consumed so that more can be made and then consumed. As the shorthand goes, "can implies ought": if we *can* buy something, we *ought* to buy it.

In his 1927 *Encyclopædia Britannica* article, "Mass Production," Henry Ford explained that mass production is what makes mass consumption possible. He made a significant point. The unsustainable culture of mass consumption that has now gone global is the *product* of mass production, not its source. The efficiencies of mechanical method create the goods which then somehow need to be consumed, so that the system can produce even more goods at yet higher efficiencies.

One of the other elements that has thus crept into culture as a consequence of prescriptive technology is an obsession with measurement. If systems are designed with efficiency in mind – whether that is in units produced per hour, or the lower cost (and thus higher profit) of mass produced goods – there needs to be some system of measurement.

At its extreme, we find the late nineteenth-century scientific management principles of Frederick Winslow Taylor ("Taylorism"), in which everything down to the number of motions required to fill boxcars was carefully measured and noted to train more efficient workers. Under the guise of "time and motion studies," the metricality of prescriptive systems has been constantly enhanced as a way of monitoring their effectiveness and improving their efficiency. Today, monitoring programs count the number of keystrokes per hour of data entry operators or time how rapidly an order is filled at a drive-thru window. It is telling social commentary that the first depiction of closed circuit television in the movies (*Modern Times*) showed surveillance of machine operation and the productivity of workers – with Charlie Chaplin getting caught smoking in the washroom on his break.

The hidden side to a culture focused on consumption and compliance is that both activities are embedded in an exchange economy.

Prescriptive systems require exchange in order to function; mass consumption depends on a variety of ways in which consumers can acquire the items they wish to consume. If the system is going to continue to function, consumers have to be as compliant in their personal lives as they are at work.

The various points or reward programs in which we are continually enrolled serve to track our consumption patterns, not only supporting inventory control and just-in-time delivery but enabling manufacturers and retailers to measure the effectiveness of various advertising and motivational strategies. Add the metrical identity generated through social media and trackable by various computer analytics, and an astonishingly detailed profile of any individual can be generated through the internet, with little effort.

The problem, of course, is that the numbers become associated with social and cultural value. Who we are, metrically, becomes what we are worth. What most needs to change if we are to reimagine a sustainable world is the dominance of the "metrical Me."

This is not a new problem. By the interwar

period, it came to characterize the attitudes embedded in the methodical, mechanical worldview. Where Raymond Fosdick warned about the loss of individuality thanks to the spread of standardization, Henri Frankfort claimed the human relationship with Nature had changed from the traditional "I/Thou" to the modern "I/It." Martin Buber (*I and Thou*) presented this in theological terms, just as George Orwell (in *1984*) and Aldous Huxley (*Brave New World*) depicted it in literary terms.

A fascination with "the metrical Me" leads inevitably to the metricalization of all things related to individual identity and to the commodification of our value as individual human beings. Quality, apart from Quantity, becomes incomprehensible, spawning the mental collapse of anyone who tries, like the protagonist in Robert Pirsig's *Zen and the Art of Motorcycle Maintenance*, to understand what it means to pursue Quality within the parameters of a metrical universe.

Yet if an unsustainable culture reflects metricality, commodification or Quantity, reimagining a sustainable world requires us to affirm an understanding of value based upon Quality. This is not a return to the past in order to find a sustainable future. It is a rediscovery of traditional wisdom to help us frame in sustainable terms what we know today about ourselves and our universe.

The most important of those principles, in response to "the metrical Me," is that a life is a life, however and wherever it is lived. There is no hierarchy of value inherent in life.

This is why I have always liked the aboriginal tradition of the talking stick. Simple or ornately carved in whatever style, it grounds a tradition of respect that a sustainable world needs both to appreciate and adopt. The tradition requires that, as the group sits in a circle, the talking stick is passed from person to person. Whoever holds the stick commands the respect and attention of the group for as long as he or she desires, to say whatever needs to be said.

I have watched how this simple act changes a group dynamic, as quiet or shy people – or perhaps those whose command of language is not as strong – blossom into contributors. Sometimes nothing at all is said – the person holds the stick, the group is silent waiting for what they might say, and then with a gesture or a polite comment, the opportunity is declined for now. Because the stick moves in a circle, it will always come back another time. The number of words that are spoken does not matter; what matters is the wisdom – the value – to the group as a whole in what is being said.

The respect that comes from waiting one's turn, the necessity of thinking before speaking, the realization that the quietest person in the group might have the most important things to say – these build community. In a circle, no one is more important than anyone else, and the talking stick reinforces the concept as it moves around.

By contrast, the metrical view ascribes a series of metrics to each of us. Some of them are obvious – height, weight, eye colour, age, the physical attributes of our identity. Others are less obvious – our country of origin, our citizenship, our bank balance. The individual is at the centre of each measurement, independent of the metrics assigned to other individuals. We are very much a culture concerned about the "I" and our metrics reflect this.

Of course, once you start measuring people, some will have higher or lower numbers than others. The process of measurement itself results in a hierarchy of metrics. Some of us are older, taller, or thinner than others, and that is the way life happens to be. There is nothing wrong with this kind of comparison, unless it shifts sideways from metrical description into a hierarchy of value. In the natural world, there is no hierarchy of value – everything has its place and is equally necessary. In the web of life that is the Earth, no single life has more inherent value than any other.

In a metrical universe, however, value is not found in relation; it is intrinsic to the individual. Some people have better metrics than others. Even when dollars are not attached, metrics of all sorts establish the value of one individual's life in relation to others. From a sustainability perspective, this cannot be allowed to happen. Whatever the metrical difference between people, the value of a life needs to be seen as equivalent wherever it is lived. We should not view the death of child in a Sudanese refugee camp with any less outrage and anger than that of a child in our own community. Given that the Sudanese child likely died of starvation while too many of our children suffer from obesity, the moral imperative to do something about it gets stronger.

While we might learn to value people equally, the larger lesson is that it is not only about valuing the lives of human beings. Anthropocentrism may exist in our heads, but the world does not share it – Gaia exists for herself, not as a stage for humans to strut across, proclaiming their superior importance.

In the end, it is a matter of respect. The value of any life is found in interdependence and relationship. In fact, the idea of independence is a relatively recent fiction in Western culture that has spread, like a destructive meme, around the world, leaving the effects of unsustainable choices in its wake.

If we extend the idea of the talking stick to the circle of Earth itself, what might the voices of other Life-bearers say to us if we only took the time to listen? If we do not respect their message, we put both our own future, and theirs, at risk. It's a good discipline. Traditions that believe the spirits speak or the gods communicate, traditions in which God or Yahweh or Allah has a voice that needs to be heard, require moments of silence. Otherwise the noise we create drowns out any potential message.

Our value is not simply in being human, but in using our humanity to value the life with which we share the whole planet. Whatever the metrics of disadvantage, economic or otherwise, an ethical system founded on any other principle than the equality of life is doomed to create disaster. A "reverence for life," in Albert Schweitzer's words, requires us to listen with respect to what life is saying as creatures of all sorts continue to create a world that large, clumsy animals like us might eventually inherit. It leads to wisdom and understanding, helping us notice patterns and relationships that we would otherwise overlook.

It's good to make causal connections, to see where one part fits into another and why, but it is misleading and potentially dangerous to think any great wisdom results from such a linear understanding of causality. It is certainly not a path that leads to a sustainable future. We can't begin to understand ecological systems in simple, linear terms. When we conceive of sustainability in a planetary context, we also need to understand nature, culture and society as complex, dynamic interrelated systems.

At this point, however, the philosophical and methodological navigation system of Western science and technology seizes up and refuses to provide any further assistance. Our cultural GPS is no help at all in providing directions toward a sustainable future. We need to recalibrate the whole system, beginning with ourselves, and to conceive of sustainability in ways that bring the Old Savage out of the Stone Age and into the twenty-first century.

ও

Interlude
Lessons from a Scrub Oak

On the prairies, trees are exotic creatures. Very few of the trees that dot the landscape as windbreaks for farmhouses are native. Stately spruce, spindly pine, the majestic elm trees that line city streets – they are all from somewhere else. Cultivated over many years now, they grow green and tall, having learned over time to thrive in prairie soil and weather.

Given a choice, however, I prefer the scrub oak, one of the few trees that seems to have roots in the prairie. It is never very large; it grows so slowly that its age is hard to determine even from the rings. It will never have the majesty of the English oak that launched the Royal Navy, or the even grain of the white and red oak that turn into beautiful floors and furniture. Knotted, gnarly, never growing too long in any one direction, the scrub oak is their misshapen cousin – in the same family, but not worth much attention.

Looking at the Earth from a different vantage point, however, and considering the lessons we can learn from what is all around us, we can learn a great deal from the scrub oak.

I grew up on five acres of Manitoba prairie, next to the Red River, in a yard full of trees of all kinds. Over time, as the poplars flourished and died, the pines grew more gaunt, the elms were lost to Dutch elm disease, and the Manitoba maples lost limbs, the oaks just grew. Slowly.

Always dwarfed by the spruce, the scrub oaks sank their roots deeper into the soil. A windstorm might pull the root ball of a tall tree out of the ground, but it could not topple the oaks. They were there to stay, and even the most violent storms stripped only bits of dead branches. Year after year, the acorns dropped. Squirrels fought over them, and scurried them away into places promptly forgotten. So, while the nuisance elms and poplars seeded everywhere to no purpose, and the spruce and pine trees scattered fruitless seeds to moulder in the dirt, the small oaks grew. Slowly.

You can tell the age of a woodlot by the kinds of trees that it contains. The old lots, the ones with a local ecosystem going back many years – likely before settlers disturbed the prairie grass – are full of scrub oak.

Moving back to Manitoba years later, my family bought a house in the same area. There are many things about this place that I would cheerfully trade, but it has trees. Mostly oaks. As the other kinds of trees planted by recent owners wax and wane, the oaks look much the same as they did fifteen years ago. According to a friend who is an expert on trees, the largest ones are easily more than 200 years old. That's long before settlers arrived in the Red River Valley, long before eager newcomers brought seeds and seedlings from somewhere else to transform what they saw as wilderness.

Every year, these trees shed acorns by the thousands. Cutting the lawn in the fall requires nerves of a warrior, because the acorns and their pieces ricochet like bullets off any solid surface.

Squirrels congregate from miles around, it seems, scurrying acorns off to places that make no sense (like clothes dryer vents and furnace intakes), but mostly planting them in prairie soil.

Every spring and summer, the oak trees spring up. I have fought a losing battle against the acorns in my raised garden beds, because it seems that a month after my own vegetables sprout, the acorns buried by squirrels a year or two earlier pound their way through in a fist of green growth, right in the middle of everything. Pulling them out is next to impossible. They have to be dug. The spindly oak tree four inches out of the ground with a few green leaves has a root from its tiny acorn that goes down well more than a foot. The explosive power to survive that drives such roots into the dry prairie soil is truly remarkable.

I have often wanted to dig up some of these seedlings, to find some patch of prairie and just plant a forest of oak trees. It would be a sign of hope for the future, because I would never live to see that forest. Nor would the next three generations. In a hundred years or so, these scrub oaks would start to look a little like the trees I remember sitting under as a child. Knowing more about the scrub oak, however, it might be better to plant the acorns themselves.

For all their resilience, the one thing these scrub oak trees can't tolerate is having the soil around their roots dug up or disturbed. Dig around an oak tree, even a few feet from its trunk, and you will leave scars in its growth that an expert can instantly identify, for a very long time.

Scrub oaks plant their roots deep in their community. They are planted there to stay. Seasons come and go, dry and wet, winds blow hard or softly through their few branches, but the scrub oaks continue. Parasites and insects infest them, but a symbiosis seems to develop that allows the scrub oak to live when other trees would have their vitality sapped.

The leaves tend to stay close to where they fall, heavy and apparently designed not to blow far in the wind. They resist rotting, so over time in a scrub oak bush – a kind of prairie peat moss – develops, helping trap moisture and nourish the trees themselves. Scrub oak leaves are the last to come out in the spring – past the point of any frost – but are also the last to surrender to the cold as winter approaches, taking advantage of every last fall day to put energy away for future growth.

As the shifting climate changes the prairies, there will be changes to the vegetation. New trees will grow; old ones will develop new diseases and be stressed by different weather. But I suspect that the one sign of continuity on the prairie landscape will be that scrub oak.

Resilience. Deep roots. The optimism of acorns formed every year, without fail, trusting in other hands to carry them away to fertile soil, where they will also sink deep roots, digging deep down into what will nourish them before reaching up for the sunlight.

Intimately related to everything in its surroundings, feeling deeply everything that affects what is close to it. Withstanding extremes of weather and wind, growing only a little in some seasons but trusting that the next one will be better. Managing extreme heat or bitter cold, dry years and wet, all with equanimity.

Preferring the company of other trees, but able to live alone, still producing the seeds that – in the long cycle of time – will pass its inheritance on to generation after generation. Taking care of its immediate home, nourishing its own roots and not depending for its survival on the attentions of others.

A shelter for birds, a home for the squirrels who chatter from its branches, shade for a person to sit and think.

Lessons from a scrub oak, toward choosing a sustainable future for ourselves and all of the children of Earth.

PART 2

᪥

Toward a Gift
Ecology

4. What Is Given, What Is Gift

Reimagining a sustainable world depends on understanding the difference between what is given and what is Gift.

For each of us, our encounter with the universe began with the gift of life. We did not ask for it, we did not deserve it, but the gift was given anyway. With the first gulp of air in our lungs, one could say, we accepted this gift, whatever else might follow.

Beyond the moment of birth, however, it is only as we enter into relationship with the world around us that we encounter the rest of what is given: those aspects of life over which we have no control, the preconditions that shape our physical and social existence.

Every culture has its own version of the given conditions of life. In aboriginal cultures, this has often been represented in terms of the medicine wheel – which of course is not a wheel, and represents wisdom rather than any healing practice. The medicine wheel divides into four quadrants, each with a corresponding colour. The quadrants represent the four directions, the four seasons, the four stages of life and the circle within which all living things move.

In ancient Greek culture and its philosophical descendants, there were the four elements – earth, air, water and fire – along with their corresponding humours, aligned by the seasons under the sphere of the moon in ways that shaped the lives of humans and all living creatures.

Every culture describes life in the language of cycles, of recurrence, of harmony – a balance that is achieved only through acceptance of what is given. In the wisdom of Ecclesiastes, "to everything there is a season, a time for everything under the sun." In Hindu cosmology, the cycle of birth and rebirth embodies the karma or destiny within which all living things dance but from which no one can escape.

What is given is therefore important, but it is not everything that is important. Balance requires us to understand how what is given shapes the world in which we live, but we must not be trapped by it as we consider ways to reimagine a sustainable future.

Humans are not merely passive recipients. The difference between humans and animals is reflected in the new possibilities we are able to create through our capacity to give, by our own choice and for our own reasons.

Animals can make choices, too, but their choices – whether they are beyond the instinctual level or not – fall within the larger pattern of what is given. Humans alone are able to step outside that pattern and – spontaneously and unpredictably, by what they give and by what they receive – to change it.

To unpack the significance of this point, we should begin with what is concrete.

We live in a world of given things, objects whose existence shapes the space within which we live and within which we make decisions.

The first category of given things consists of the material objects with which we are constantly engaged: our physical bodies and what those bodies require for health – food, water, air, shelter. The scale of basic needs can be extended for social and cultural reasons, but there is a definable minimum that physical survival requires.

Beyond this is the world we have created, the stuff of our lives that surrounds us daily, like possessions buried with the dead in an ancient tomb. We live in a dynamic museum of the stuff that shapes our desires, our activities, our work, our leisure, our anxieties. These things become physical and material dimensions of our identity, which is why a disaster, like a fire or a tornado, that destroys our possessions can be so overwhelming.

There are also given things that differ for each generation in each different place, given material conditions. We deal with water scarcity in some places, too much water in others. Some people build against earthquakes, others dig down against tornados, still others plan evacuation and sea walls against hurricanes and typhoons. If you live, as I do, in a cold part of Canada, plan to have warm clothes in the winter and bug spray to counter mosquitoes in the summer.

All these things shape our living spaces and affect our daily decisions, but they do not determine either where or how we live.

In the context of sustainability, we are also presented with a litany of given things. That is the essence of envirometrics, which gives us the numbers as they are now and projects where they are headed according to a linear and mechanical view of systems, including planetary ones. These are the metrics of Earth, of Gaia, the measurement that our methods provide about the given conditions of the planet at any particular time.

In part, this is necessary; it provides a baseline of realism as we discuss choices toward a sustainable world. What are the metrics of pollution of the air, water, earth? How many people exist, and where? What do they consume? Where are natural resources available, and how much, and for how long? How many cars are there, how much oil and gas do they consume, what do they really cost? Everything from the rate at which glaciers are melting, to how quickly sea levels are rising, to the changing global temperature gradient, is important for us to know.

These kinds of metrics can help us to effect policy change or to plan for the consequences of climate change – provided everything is counted and displayed. If the price per barrel of oil on the world market is measured, but not the actual costs of production or the environmental costs of consumption, then the metrics are serving some purpose other than guiding choices toward a sustainable future. Selective metrics are an old political and economic game in which the objective is to manipulate the outcome, not provide an objective view.

We need to know what is given, but we also need to know why and to what purpose. However much we owe to the four directions or the four elements, there is more to the universe than what the wind blows our way or what we find beneath our feet. If we focus only on the things that are given, we do not see other possibilities that a gift might create.

Consider the nature of a gift. Whoever accepts a gift also accepts the unexpected possibilities it embodies. A gift changes everything, precisely because it is something whose appearance a mechanical system cannot predict and whose dynamic effects cannot be anticipated.

Mechanical systems do not handle uncertainty and possibility very well, if at all. Sometimes measurements are only possible by suspending the dynamic – you can have either speed or position, but not both at the same moment. Other variables can be tracked only if the other system variables are turned into constants – the famous dilemma of "if all other things are equal," when they never are.

Add complexity to a system, or make it into one that is interdependent and dynamic, with an infinite number of variables, and no predictable result outside of a cloud of probabilities is possible. A certain degree of redundancy and flexibility may be designed into systems, but no mechanical system would ever be able to include in its design parameters the human capacity for spontaneous response.

The supercomputer Deep Blue, which was able to play chess well enough to beat grandmasters, had to calculate the probabilities by playing ahead to discover the multiplicity of outcomes from any one particular possible move. If it takes a massive supercomputer to calculate the movement of sixteen pieces on a sixty-four-square board, imagine the impossibility of ever scaling something up in similar linear, mechanical fashion to predict the outcomes of environmental decisions on a planetary scale – much less ones involving humans in their widely divergent versions of society and culture.

Throw into this mix the wildly unpredictable and exuberant possibilities of a spontaneous Gift, and such a predictive system is bound to implode.

We cannot ignore the metrics involved in reimagining a sustainable world, however. Whether we like it or want it or not, the givenness of any one thing, like the givenness of any colour on the medicine wheel, is there by its nature. Given things become the fixed points around which our decisions swirl, the objects and tools by which we implement our choices. Given things symbolize those values that are reflected in what we choose to do in our lives together. They need to be recognized and inventoried, their places noted and the values inherent in their origins, their design, their construction and their use identified. Then we need to move forward, making the dynamic changes that rearrange the stuff of our lives into new patterns to nudge society and culture in a sustainable direction.

It is interesting how givenness is easier to see in our stuff than in our values. Each generation also has certain attitudes and values that are passed on from generation to generation. They may be like water to a fish, but they are present all the same. When that aspect of givenness is not recognized, then we are unable to respond appropriately to new or dynamic situations. At some point the material aspect of "what is given" is hard to dodge because it is material – like the need for clean water to drink. If we don't have clean water, then what is "given" becomes obvious, and we will manage it as best we can. But attitudes and values are products of culture and manifested in society like anything we have chosen to make or do. They can also seem more intractable and determinate than in fact they are.

From the time the Old Savage first used a rock as a tool, human attitudes and values have created culture and shaped society just as they, in turn, have been created and shaped. When we speak of some natural state of "givenness," therefore, the only creature on the planet *unable* to use the four directions as an excuse for not doing things differently is the Old Savage. Whatever the constraints of his physical circumstances, the Old Savage is the only creature with the capacity to make moral choices that change what is given into something new and different through the spontaneity of a Gift.

Attitudes and values are present by choice, not by necessity. Should humans recognize the need to make changes to those attitudes and values, they will be changed – in the blink of an eye – and different reasons for new choices will appear. Of all the metrics of an unsustainable world, therefore, the one set of metrics that could be changed overnight is the attitudes and values of the human population.

Recall what was said about the nature of technology in the prelude to this book: We live in a world of our own choosing. It is the result of choices we have made, individually and collectively. We can make different choices – if we want to. In our time, we are often frightened by talk of autonomous technology, the image of the runaway train moving faster and faster, with no one driving it, heading for disaster. This is nonsense. Technology is not neutral. Technology may seem like a given thing, but it is not – it is a product of our choices. Technology is in our heads, not in our hands.

Some aspects of technology seem given. We are not likely to be successful using a loaf of bread as a hammer, or using a hammer to make an omelette – but even those aspects are embedded by humans who have chosen to make something in a certain way for certain reasons. Each object in our personal or social space is the result of choices someone else made before we entered the picture. We can acquiesce and copy their choices, or we can make new ones of our own that reflect other attitudes and values.

One response to sustainability – a response that offers a siren call to our consumer society – is the idea that there could be a "green economy," that there is (as in Paul Hawken's book) an "ecology of commerce." The problem, of course, is that "green" can be as much a commodity as anything else. If the problem is, as I argue, the exchange economy itself, then it doesn't matter much what is exchanged, however noble the reason. The idea of a green economy provides no more than a convenient "green-washing" of the attitudes and values that have created the problem in the first place; it does not restore the balance between what is given and what is Gift.

To reimagine a sustainable world, we need to be inspired by what the Old Savage has understood from the earliest civilization to the present – the idea of the Gift, and how it is both offered and received within a universe of relations. The Gift requires us to consider not just the four directions, but also the other three directions, which provide the context of what a gift might mean:

We look up, and encounter the Creator or Source of the universe, and all the life and possibilities within it. We look down, and encounter the Earth on which we stand and within whose life we are inescapably entwined. We look inside, and in a moment of self-recognition, encounter the essence of what truly lies in our hearts.

Thus, while we live in a world full of given things, some of our own choosing and making, we also live in a world in which what is given is much less powerful than we think.

Numbers and statistics are limiting – they demarcate the boundaries of mass culture and the likely behaviour of its members, but they are far from absolute. Apply these social metrics to any one person, and the statistics (which are always about probabilities, not certainties, anyway) do not necessarily apply. Define a person by their personal metrics – by age, for example – and listen to the doors close, but not for everyone who shares those same characteristics.

Whether you are a woman or a man, gender shapes not only who you are but what choices and options you have – but it doesn't *determine* those choices and options, even if it makes some more difficult than others. Add economic factors, money, social position, education, race, sexual orientation, and each set of definitions creates boundaries and horizons for the possible – but does not make them inviolate.

We still make choices, and the most transformational choice we can make is to give a gift to someone else – unexpected, unanticipated and unforeseen. The second most transformational choice we can make is to accept such a gift, to allow the relationship that it symbolizes to change who we are and the systems within which we are located.

We need to restore a balance between what is given and what is Gift. The concept of exchange and the commodification of what is exchanged go back to early civilization. Yet it has only been since the Renaissance and the rise of industrial culture that such an exchange has encompassed all of the elements of our existence and spread to every dimension of the planet, above and below its surface.

What we have lost, as a result, is the concept of the Gift – not an exchange, not something requiring reciprocity (going back and forth, like a machine), but a gift, freely and generously given as an expression both of self and of relation. A gift embodies change, difference and possibility, rearranging what is given in the dynamism of the new relationship the gift initiates.

What I suggest, therefore, is not that we must dispose of the exchange economy altogether, but that the balance must be restored between the necessities of exchange and the opportunities of gifting. The key element is not the object or the process, but the intention, the attitude – what emerges from our understanding of what lies inside and beyond the daily round of our transactions.

We cannot go "back to the future" to find this difference. Ethnographic depictions of the "gift economy" found among so-called primitive cultures at the dawn of the twentieth century are inadequate examples of how we should reimagine a sustainable world. The culture of exchange is not new, nor is it only manifested only in the more elaborate versions of civilization that the Old Savage has chosen to construct. Any historic culture that had slaves or social classes embedded commodification in how it was structured and managed, regardless of how the exchange took place.

We need to step outside of the exchange relationship into a universe of relations in order to understand how to balance what is given with what we may give or accept as Gift. We need a new synthesis of everything we have learned if we are to achieve such a balance and thus enable the Old Savage to grow into the New Civilization we have created before it is too late.

5. A Universe of Relations

Michael Faraday was as much a threat to the Mechanicians of his own time as he is to their philosophical descendants today. With the mechanical, Newtonian worldview yet to be challenged by the rise of quantum physics and relativity theory, Faraday's discovery of the unifying relationship between electricity and magnetism was more the result of belief than of Method.

Faraday was a Christian, or more precisely a Sandemanian, a follower of the Protestant sect founded by John Glas and his son-in-law, Robert Sandeman. Faraday disliked the way mathematics had unfolded into the calculus of motion. He believed God had made the universe beautiful and symmetrical, full of simple underlying relations that merely had to be uncovered – and so he uncovered them.

Had he shown as much interest in mathematics as he did in chemistry and physics, Faraday would no doubt have crowed with delight at the realization that Euclidean geometry, long seen to be a description of the actual nature of the universe, was little more than a human assertion of one particular set of axioms, not any divine intention or design. The underlying symmetry of God's universe could no more be scribed on a piece of paper than a rainbow could be captured in a jar.

Once the principles of electromagnetism had been discovered, of course, the Methodists took over and furiously attempted to render them part of the mechanisms already in place, but Faraday's discovery was a disquieting precursor of the annihilation of the Newtonian universe by a Swiss patent office clerk named Albert Einstein.

For Faraday, it was obvious that we live in a universe of relations, not merely an environment of connections. That those relations were spiritual as well as physical, emotional as well as philosophical, was something he felt no need to justify or explain.

۽

We live simultaneously in two universes –the metrical and the non-metrical, the universe that can be counted and measured and the universe that can't. Everything of value is in the non-metrical universe.

It is not a new idea to say humans live in more than one place. Sir Thomas Browne's famous depiction of Man in *Religio Medici* (1643) – as "that great and true Amphibium" able to move between two worlds – reflects a dichotomy that has plagued Western thought for a long time.

To say that the split got worse with René Descartes's *Discourse on the Method,* and then with what is fondly described as "the rise of modern science," would be an understatement. Yet what is most troubling is not the dichotomy (whether between body and spirit, faith and reason, or mind and matter), but that one side of the equation increasingly seems to be left off the page. For a sustainable future, this has to change.

Browne and his contemporaries had great philosophical and religious debates on the dichotomy in human experience. In various forms, those debates carried on into the beginning of the twentieth century. In the beginning of the twenty-first century, however, such public debates are no longer mainstream. Instead they are likely to be found in the cloisters of religious institutions, among groups of those already convinced of the answer. In public, secularism holds sway. Religious or spiritual concerns are at best private and at worst are evidence of a lapse in critical thinking and judgment, not to be shared.

Such conclusions are both flawed and dangerous, but for now I want to focus on a different dichotomy, spawned by the physical sciences at the start of the twentieth century, which continues to unfold.

The development of Einsteinian physics in its various forms – whether relativity or quantum theory – did more than supplant Newtonian physics. Whereas in the world of normal sense experience Newtonian mechanics continued to be used and valued, when it came down to issues about "matter," much doubt was expressed about the fundamental nature of reality – but from a scientific as opposed to a religious perspective. A dichotomy, at the least, was asserted between mind and matter. As matter became less substantial, however, the dismissal of mind as a subject fit for scientific investigation became less convincing.

When Arthur Eddington (later knighted for his role in demonstrating the general theory of relativity through an investigation of the 1919 solar eclipse) gave the Gifford Lectures published in 1928 as *The Nature of the Physical World*, he commanded both attention and respect – at least until he got to the end of his argument. After an authoritative and succinct statement of the nature of the universe, Eddington drew out the implications of claiming that Einsteinian physics made matter insubstantial. Titling those last four chapters "Pointer Readings," "Reality," "Causation" and "Science and Mysticism," Eddington drove home the crucial point: in relation to the fundamental properties of matter and the nature of reality, science was not far off saying the sorts of things found in mysticism. It caused enough of a furor that, the following year, Eddington (also a Quaker) published his Swarthmore Lecture as *Science and the Unseen World*, trying to elaborate on the idea.

Eddington cleverly sidestepped the problem of providing proof for the "unseen world" by going after the concept of reality itself. The observable universe, especially as revealed through science and daily experience, could be counted and measured. He referred to it as a universe of "pointer readings." It was a universe of appearance, if quantum physics was to be believed, even if it was observationally and practically "real." Calling this "the metrical universe," he set it against the "non-metrical universe," which could be neither counted nor measured. The non-metrical universe contains all those aspects of life that can be observed only in their effects. Chief among this was mind – the universe, he said, was made of "mind stuff." Through modern physics, Eddington helped to revive what Browne and his contemporaries had expressed in their debates. Humans don't face a dichotomy between mind and matter; we live in both universes simultaneously.

Across most traditions, a robust religious life requires integration and synthesis of beliefs with actions, seeing evidence in the metrical universe of pointer readings of the reality of the non-metrical universe of mind – and of value. "Either/ or" is an unacceptable attitude – it needs to be "both/and" instead. It is not a dichotomy, but a duality.

We live in both universes, simultaneously. The metrical universe is the world of daily experience in which Newtonian mechanics holds sway; we do not jump off bridges or walk in front of trucks without knowing exactly what will happen and why. Yet the universe of thoughts, feelings, beliefs, emotions and passions is where we live as human beings. Everything of value is found in the non-metrical universe, and when we lose sight of this, we become less than human. One of the reasons it is so hard for sustainability to gain ground, one of the reasons the Old Savage remains oblivious to the effects of his tools, is that the non-metrical universe of value is ignored and discounted. We need to reclaim the public space for a discussion of all the dimensions of human experience.

Economic measures persistently trump any other kind of analysis. We might pay lip service to the idea that every human life is precious and of incalculable value, but in the choices we routinely make, we put a price on life, for a variety of material reasons. We live amongst the pointer readings, by the rise and fall of currency markets and stock exchanges, GDP, GNP, unemployment rates and trade imbalances. We trade in future pork bellies without asking ourselves whether anyone wants pork, or whether it can be supplied, or whether it is good for the planet. Certainly no one is concerned about what the pigs might think of all this.

Sustainability requires us to consider not just whether we can do something, but whether we should, and why, and for reasons that go beyond what can be counted and measured.

Sustainability requires us to realign ourselves with the universe of values, with the non-metrical universe in which what is important can never be weighed, commodified, calculated, measured or exchanged.

Our awareness of the non-metrical universe is found in the ways we are able to annihilate the distance that a metrical world asserts between us and other people, between us and the Earth, and between us and our understanding of what the universe means as a whole. The annihilation of distance is, however, a negative idea; the positive one involves instead the celebration of Presence.

ॐ

Distance is an uneasy concept. Engineers and architects, carpenters and plumbers — those who live and work in the metrical universe – have no trouble with it at all. Nor do physicists who explore the inner reaches of the atom, even as they use measurements meaningless in the larger world. Distance in every other sense, however, is uneasy. We can travel from point A to point B, knowing when we left, how far we travelled, the route we took and when we arrived. Yet when we step outside of this metrical framework, everything material – arrival and departure, route and destination, and whatever else the journey involved – becomes meaningless.

The real annihilation of distance is found between two people. It has little to do with physical proximity, because time and space – those characteristics of the metrical universe – are irrelevant. People together in the here and now can be separated by infinite distance; people separated not only by distance but in time can be present in memory and in thought, shaping the intimate details of each other's lives in ways that can be observed though not explained.

Presence and the gift of Presence step outside

time and space. This language seems spiritual because it tries to symbolize the dimension of our lives that is lived in the non-metrical universe. It is the universe of value, in which nothing can be counted and measured, where we find everything that is important to us.

Mesmerized by our wired world with its electronic links, we can begin to think that with enough connections, everything will come alive, as it did in old science fiction stories such as Robert Heinlein's *The Moon is a Harsh Mistress*. If only there are enough switches, the computer will become more than an artificial intelligence. It will make the mystical leap into something that not only thinks but feels.

Yet we live in a universe of relations, not an environment of connections. Electronic means allow us to connect to people all over the world, instantly appearing in devices in places where we may never go, communicating with people we may never meet in person. The friendships created and maintained, the wisdom and feelings that are shared, the lives that are shaped through these connections, can and do change the world. But it is not the connections that make the difference in who we are as human beings. It is the relations.

From the moment of our birth, we are separated from every other person by what can seem like an unbridgeable abyss. In our wired world, we communicate from inside our own pod, increasingly insulated from the social relationships with other people that were common even a generation ago. We communicate nothing much of who we really are, but we can do it very quickly, and at a great distance. If there is one emotional barrier to creating a sustainable future, it is the loneliness of too many people who feel no one cares and so care little themselves. In the universe of relations, however, all that can change in a moment.

In the end, humans live in the skin, not in the etherworld of electrons and tweets. There is no substitute for that moment of shared recognition that creates Presence between two people who have never met before, that instant of relation that annihilates everything in between. After such a moment – whether achieved in the letters of another era or in the phone calls and instant messages of today – this

Presence is called to mind and grounds whatever is communicated.

With the right words, distance can be annihilated between two people who may rarely have the chance to sit across the table and eat a simple meal together, debating who gets the last spring roll. With the right words, an intimacy in spirit can be called to life. With the right words, time becomes inconsequential as memories bring the past literally to life inside of us.

L.M. Montgomery's Anne of Green Gables would gush extravagantly about meeting "a kindred spirit," someone with whom that instant rush of recognition went beyond the immediate and physical into some spiritual dimension, where friendship and intimacy are instantaneous and forever. In the connected environment, with our urge for more Facebook friends or links or contacts, we cast a net worldwide in search of such kindred spirits, hoping as we search the electronic world that we can find Presence and not feel alone.

In such a mechanical search-at-a-distance for relationship, however, we no longer see what is close at hand – opportunities to meet the eyes of those who would otherwise pass us by as strangers. We substitute the constructed realities of our connections for the present realities of the people we meet. It is an artificial world, one that we have built according to our expectations, full of what we think we need and perhaps a little of what lies aching in our hearts. There is activity, but no Presence.

People are messy and unexpected. They upset calculations and plans, they interrupt our contemplations and disrupt the order we are compelled to seek. But in a universe of value, where it seems we most fear being alone, we must struggle to be Present with each person we meet.

It is hard to do this, because it takes care, wisdom and empathy to bridge the gulf between two people. We need to be where we are, to search not an internet of connections but the eyes of strangers, people who are brought into our path by a pattern not of our making or choosing, for what we most need ourselves to find. As we do this, we give a gift to everyone who meets us, everyone who sees in our eyes the recognition of a common moment of shared time together. In that moment without words, who we are is communicated to the other person, and – sometimes, and without forewarning or logic – we ourselves experience that gift of Presence, after which we are separated only by the mereness of space.

❧

Years ago, before his work was allowed to circulate in more than typescript among his friends and colleagues, I encountered the ideas of the Passionist priest Thomas Berry in what became a turning point in my own personal journey. A battle-scarred Protestant, I fiercely contested philosophical ground against a bevy of Roman Catholic nuns in one of my graduate courses, to the utter dismay of the professor/priest, who was trying to share Berry's covert message of wholeness and reconciliation. To everyone's surprise, especially my own, we eventually found such a consensus at a deeper and more profound level than any of us had expected.

When I think therefore of a universe of relations, of our need to understand our human story in the larger context – not only of the Earth story, but the story of the universe itself – I am drawn back to the work of Thomas Berry. Here, in this particular book, I am going no further than to say that in a universe of relations, a feeling of Presence with the Earth does not depend on where we are, but on who we are. Whether we are in a city teeming with asphalt or awash in the scent of diesel exhaust or sitting under a tree contemplating some last wilderness unscarred by human ambition, we can experience a feeling of Presence with the Earth. The only barrier to that feeling is what lies inside our own minds.

Similarly, in a universe of relations, encountering the Presence of the Creator, the Source of life and meaning, is something that also depends on who we are, not where. Suffice it to say that, in a world where other values are espoused by the disciples of Mechanism and of Method, the personal lives of many people are still shaped and directed by such encounters.

In all three of these instances of Presence – with other people, with the Earth, and with the spiritual Source of the universe – we are reminded of values other than those found in a world of objects and commodities, manipulated and consumed within the mechanisms of economic exchange. Reimagining a sustainable

world requires us to think beyond what is given –
to what we have received as Gift ourselves and to
what we are able to share as Gift with others.

ॐ

6. Gift Ecology:
Rebalancing Ecology and Economy

The alternative to an exchange is a gift.

This is a simple and obvious idea. Its implications, however, take us back to the beginning of everything, to the start of life in the universe, to the beginning of our own.

Examine every mythology and you will find that life – including human life – is never the result of a transaction. It is a gift, whose consequences unfold into the people whose origins are found in such a gesture. Life may be a gift misused, and those who receive it may not be worthy of the gift, but it is a gift all the same.

A gift required or expected is not a gift. By nature, a gift entails choice, not obligation or compulsion. This is a good thing, because what is of greatest value to us is something for which we have nothing to exchange.

We hear often about the "gift of friendship," but it would pervert friendship to see it as an exchange. Friendship may display a cycle of giving and receiving, each friend giving what the other needs at the moment, but its dynamic nature means that calculation and expectation undermine rather than strengthen the relationship.

We also hear about the gift of one's time, usually in financial campaigns, as an alternative to the money that is initially sought. These campaigns entirely miss the point. I can always calculate what my financial donation will cost, but the value of my time is, quite literally, priceless. Time, after all, is itself a gift. None of us knows how much we have, and many people have left this world wishing they had more or had used it more wisely. Turn it into something requiring an exchange, however, and we have wages, per hour, for jobs done.

If you are looking for an explanation, in a nutshell, of why pride in one's work is less than it was or why there is so little artistry in the things we create in our civilization – even our art – it is because of the most damnable of all equations: Time = Money. A craftsman works at something until it is right, until it reflects his intention and his vision for its completion. Even if it must be finished before it is "done," whatever regret this incompletion causes is matched by pride in what was accomplished and resolution that the next piece will be better.

Despite all our technological accomplishments, we build bridges that last twenty-five years, bringing materials from a great distance in transport trucks for their construction – travelling over roads and bridges built nearly two thousand years ago by Roman labourers with hand tools and local materials. We marvel at the height of our skyscrapers, but look with incredulity at the detail of a ceiling mosaic in a mosque or the intricacies of a gargoyle mounted hundreds of feet in the air on a medieval cathedral.

We no longer even hand-write letters. How could we possibly understand the life-work of a monk, dedicated to completing the writing and illustration of a few pages in an illuminated manuscript? Even postcards are a rarity – collected as souvenirs of a trip, they are no longer sent to friends as a sign of the shared feeling "I wish you had been here with me." Instead, we post a Flickr stream of photos.

Creating mosaics and writing letters are examples of giving the gift of time. Why do some people feel compelled to do more than is expected of them? It's an entirely different feeling when money is received as a gift, not as compensation – out of generosity, not compelled by a collective agreement. People working to complete a project, I suspect, are happier in the end than those who simply put in the required hours to receive the compensation expected for their time.

If we were we to take a tour around the Earth in time as well as in geography, there would be myriad examples, everywhere, of how humans have focused their culture on the giving of gifts while at the same time their societies developed the medium and practice of transaction. Even when, as between strangers or leaders, there is what we have mislabelled an "exchange" of gifts (instead of "gift-giving ceremony"), the gift one chooses for the other is a measure of respect, value and worth. The well-chosen gift, valued for its appropriateness to the person who receives it and the circumstance in which it is given, is never about what it costs.

So if humans have always understood what it means to give and receive a gift, we don't need to learn new attitudes and behaviours. We just need to be reminded of why it is important.

But what is the difference between a purchase – a transaction – and a gift? To begin with, there may be no difference in what is exchanged or given – it could easily be the exact same thing. A transaction is limited by the terms of the exchange. A gift initiates or symbolizes a relationship. In a transaction, there are expectations – they might be explicit or implicit, but there are boundaries and limits to what is involved. In the giving of a gift, what is offered is undeserved and unexpected. We may try to commodify the act with a "wish list" of what we would like to receive, but this undermines the relationship that gift-giving signifies.

When a gift is offered, it can be refused, but what is refused is not just the gift itself but its signification, what it means. If a gift is offered to initiate a relationship, then the refusal of the gift is a refusal of the relationship – which is why courting gifts have always required a delicacy of discernment in all cultures back into the mist of time. One needs to be exactly sure what accepting this particular goat actually means!

Gift-giving, therefore, signifies possibility. Receiving a gift signifies accepting the possibility of the relationship that the giver intends. There are no limits, horizons or boundaries – just possibilities, which the two parties are then free to explore.

I have therefore set "gift ecology" against "exchange economy." The two terms are antithetical in every respect. Because both are found in the stuff of our lives, they may involve the same tools and opportunities, but they yield entirely different results, for radically different reasons.

To play the etymology game, it is worth remembering that in ancient philosophical contexts, the Greek word *logos* – which gave us one half of "ecology" – identifies the inherent pattern of the universe. In more frequent usage, such as in conversations about biology or technology, it is seen as a system of physical patterns or connections. Add the word *oikos,* with its reference to the household, and there is a world of difference between ecology and economics in their modern derivations.

One aspect of managing the estate's daily operations is the transactional element, which requires a firm grasp of the metrics of everything involved. Yet whenever judgments are required to maximize immediate returns or manage toward future health, metrics are less helpful than wise stewardship based upon an understanding of both the metrical and non-metrical elements. "Ecology" therefore symbolizes the web of living relationships. "Economics" is entirely about metrics; the future exists as a metrical category to be measured and weighed in terms of its probabilities.

Were we to label our gods as the Greeks did, one might say there is a world of difference between the followers of Ecology and the followers of Economics. Followers of Ecology may successfully learn to use the language and rituals of Economics without losing their souls, but the followers of Economics can never learn more than the semblance of Ecology. After all, in the metrical world of the exchange economy, "soul" is a meaningless and empty category, irrelevant to any calculation.

If we live in a universe of relations and not

merely an environment full of connections, recognizing the deeper patterns in those relations is essential to making choices toward a sustainable future. The last two hundred years in particular yield ample evidence of the disastrous unintended consequences of trying to manage the Earth by metrical means, however well intentioned. Ecology is not confined to the metrical universe of things that can be counted – frog calls per second, compared to this time last year. It is also a manifestation of the non-metrical universe of mind, meaning and value.

Pairing "gift" with "ecology," therefore, is appropriate. Giving a gift is not just a matter of metrics, either – it begins or deepens a relationship in ways that also cannot be counted or measured. In terms of sustainability, the two words together are a reminder that we need to understand deeper relationships than those that are observable through our science and technology.

Returning to the differences between ecology and economy, the first tends to be self-sustaining while the second is only theoretically sustainable. Think of it in terms of how systems work. An ecological system continually adjusts to conditions to maintain an equilibrium required for its ongoing life. Economic systems seem to require constant intervention to maintain a semblance of equilibrium over the longer term.

Economics is inherently hierarchical. Growth is measured in percentages, not in wisdom, and the prospect of death and rebirth tends not to be seen as a good thing, especially by shareholders. Success is measured in the same comparative, competitive way – a larger pile of money confers not only success, but freedom to choose what is done next with it. Within ecology, hierarchy makes no sense. Systems require all of their elements to function properly; from the smallest to the largest component, there is an interdependency that makes pointless any discussion of hierarchy. All elements of the system must be respected for their own intrinsic value if there is to be sustainability.

Gift ecology, therefore, is a self-organizing system based upon giving without any anticipated return. Its participants freely choose to offer what they have to others out of a generosity of spirit and not in response to expectation or coercion. What is offered may be material in part, but it will also be non-material, grounded in a universe of values and not only in the economic world we have designed and asserted.

It is what indigenous peoples around the world have long recognized and what they have lost, with the rest of us, in the global dominance of the exchange economy. Taking only what was needed from the world around them, they respected the spirits of the animals they used for food, acknowledged the directions of the universe and welcomed the creation that enfolded them along with everything else.

It is what every religious tradition on the planet has embedded in its culture, maintaining the centrality of spirit amidst the illusions of reality we find in the physical world around us. In all these traditions, the impulse to care is in its purest form, without expectation of any material return. It is an expression of what Albert Schweitzer murmured was a "reverence for life."

Words may be the tools we use to define and shape the world around us, but the implications of gift ecology take us out into the wilds, where anything is possible.

Gift ecology is intentional in the moment,

giving toward an end that is sustainable in the long term but not perceptible in the present. It creates spontaneous possibilities that will appear unpredictable, unmanageable and chaotic from the standpoint of any metrical exchange.

It is about feeling, about emotion, about passion – aspects of our lives as humans that find no resonance in the metrics of an exchange but which are integral within a system of relations.

It creates inspiration. It challenges us to reconceive not only the solution, but the problem itself. It compels us to throw our whole being toward creating a sustainable future for all of the children of earth, as Thomas Berry put it – not just the human ones.

It is found in the best of creativity and the triumphs of ingenuity, gifts thrown out into the universe as acts of celebration. See it in a painting, hear it in a symphony, admire it in a cathedral, mark it in the life of a da Vinci as much as in the delight of a child's first smile.

In the exchange economy, we fear to give too much and worry about where to find what we need to replace what is lost. We want to control what is given, anxious that our efforts will be wasted by those who do not appreciate what we have provided. We count the numbers, and measure the cost, and fear for a future in which the metrics are already catastrophic.

In a gift ecology, we see the same metrics but in a different context and from a different perspective. The world becomes full of possibilities as people give what they should not be able to give, or what they did not realize they had, toward a future for which there is no limit except what imagination can envision and generosity can provide. Every element, every person, has value in being, not only in being useful or profitable.

Perhaps you can see, better than I can, how the possibilities unfold from this point for how we might live together and how we might make wiser choices toward a sustainable future. What has been said here only begins to unpack what a difference it would make if gift trumped exchange, if ecology rather than economy shaped our views of what we should do, if values and emotion drove our decisions instead of profits and anticipated returns.

I spoke of restoring a balance. In a global society, there must be some means of exchange, some commodification of what is passed between people who interact at a distance. But it needs to be framed in the larger context gift ecology could provide. In the absence of gift ecology, the exchange economy will continue to propel the Earth along the devastating trajectory that we have witnessed over the past several hundred years. Something needs to change if the outcome of the system is going to be any different than, at the moment, it appears it will be.

Yet how could any of these ideas make a practical difference to the range of problems that confront us in our generation, the seemingly insurmountable barriers to a sustainable future that drive people either to despair or into denial?

"You are only one person, you can't make a difference in this larger picture, so don't bother trying. Perhaps people used to have some effect on others in their local community, but now we live in a global village, and nobody really cares about what you say or do. If it makes you feel better to recycle or compost, go ahead – but it won't change the world. Never has, never will."

In all the conversation about events on a global scale, from global warming to global overpopulation to the global economy, we have lost both our sense of personal and of historical perspective.

We have lost our sense of personal perspective because we don't see how the large-scale problems we face are, at their root, the product of small-scale and entirely personal choices by individuals.

We have lost our sense of historical perspective because we fail to recognize that no significant change, for good or ill, has ever been the result of the actions of a group. It has always been one person, making a choice, which starts the change.

That is not how history tends to be written, of course. The evidence for those individual choices is harder to find than the sweep of archival sources describing the group's actions, but the fact remains: individual choices matter. History is the larger narrative written out of individual choices.

If we want a better future, people have to make the choices that lead to it. The biggest barrier to sustainability, therefore, is the disempowerment of individuals who don't feel they can make choices of any significance at all.

If we want to reimagine a sustainable world and our relations with each other, we first need to reimagine our story. Whether we see it as the Earth Story or the Universe Story, it has to step outside the metrics of what is given into the non-metrical universe of meaning and Gift. Our lives may unfold in a trajectory in time and space, but their meaning is found in story. We are all authors as well as characters. Even minor characters can change any story. And do.

One of the more iconic stories of the last century was J.R.R. Tolkien's *Lord of the Rings* trilogy. The story was written in Britain during some of the darkest days of the early Second World War, and it has understandably been read as a symbolic narrative of where Tolkien's generation found hope. Hope was not to be found in the large events unfolding so catastrophically on all sides, but in the resilience and determination of people beneath the notice of the various social elites, people whose individual choices would turn the tide.

We live in the midst of such a story ourselves. Whether there will still be humans around to read what we have written will depend on what each of us chooses today and every day. In that sense, we are literally the authors of our own story – what we choose, what we do, what it means, how the story develops and, eventually, how it ends. That fact carries a sense of empowerment, moral agency, social responsibility and personal capacity. It also is fraught with the possibilities of the Gift.

Sweeping statements about the power of mass culture need to be identified as manipulation that renders us impotent as individuals, persuading us to act with the group and buy the latest stuff – preferably without thought – instead of choosing for ourselves. In reality, we all make ethical choices by the hundreds each day. We just need to recognize them for what they are and to think about the values that lie behind the choices we are already making. We need to see and understand what is given, but then to step past what is given to offer the new possibilities to be found in a gift if we want a sustainable world.

After all, we are not only authors in the story of our own lives. We are also at least minor characters in the story of everyone we meet. What we say and do, who we are and how we live, has a ripple effect on the lives of everyone we meet, every life we touch. On balance, I think this is where the best reason for hope is found. We are all characters. Some play bigger roles on the world stage than others, but we all have our role, however minor it may seem at the time, or how far away from the main dramatic action. The Earth story includes every living thing. Each day, we touch the lives of the people we encounter. Whether it is a small interaction or not, accidental or intentional, the pattern shifts with whatever we say or do to them.

The crucial element is the level of our engagement – whether we meet the other person's eyes, and speak to who they are, out of who we are, can make a world of difference. What we say or do can have effects beyond any expectation. When we are engaged in some way with another person, it takes us beneath the surface of trivial encounter and evokes a moment of Presence.

Philosophers have tried to articulate what happens, psychologists have tried to explain it, but it is still best expressed in the words of the storyteller, whether seated in the community circle around the night fire or hunched over a computer. When we choose to take a risk and fling ourselves out into the life of another person, even for a moment, the story changes. We ourselves become the Gift, the agent of change that transforms a static system into one that is dynamic with unanticipated possibilities.

When we take that risk and give the Gift of who we are, without thought of return and in celebration of Life itself, the story of the universe changes, too.

ॐ
Postlude
The Turtle's Gift

In the summers when we drove between our home in southern Ontario and family in Manitoba, we would pass the Straits of Mackinac. There was something about that place that drew us just to sit by the water and, when we could, to take the hydrofoil to Mackinac Island for the day.

It was only years later that I read the Ojibway legend of the Turtle's Gift, how after the Great Flood the spirit Manitou allowed the water creatures to take pity on the sky-woman and to give her a place to rest on the shell of the giant Turtle. One by one, the water animals tried to bring up dirt from the bottom in order for her to create the land once again; one by one they failed. Finally, the least of these creatures, the muskrat – after everyone thought it had died in the attempt – returned with a little bit of soil.

The sky woman placed the soil on the back of the Turtle. After the soil grew into an island, the Turtle swam away. The place became known as Michilimackinac, from which all other life on the Earth was restored.

For giving this gift, the slow-moving Turtle was made the messenger between all living creatures, physical and spiritual, swift as the thoughts that are shared among every being – a symbol of Presence in a universe of relations.

The sustainability problem reminds me of my favourite arcade game, Whac-A-Mole. Some indeterminate creature pops out of holes in a random pattern, requiring you to whack it with a mallet at an ever increasing rate until the end of the game. Blessed with good hand-eye coordination, I could always count on winning some pointless prize for whoever was with me.

When it comes to sustainability, however, the Whac-A-Mole approach will ultimately not be successful. The game will just get harder, and there is no prize at the end – because there will be no end to the creatures that pop out at us, faster and faster, until we are eventually overwhelmed.

The Old Savage needs to learn that skill and good tools will not be enough to solve the problems preventing a sustainable future. It is not a question of getting better or faster at solving the problems as they emerge, using more people and more mallets. You need to change the game itself.

Ultimately, the only way to win at planetary Whac-A-Mole is to unplug the machine – to change the conditions of the game in some way that lets you step outside the problem-solving loop. The solution is not to be found in science and technology, or in greater skill at problem-solving using such tools. The solution is a transformation in how we relate to each other and to the Earth.

If we change the game, people will find answers for themselves to the social, economic and environmental problems that a sustainable future requires. We need to transform the culture of unsustainability that continues to create these problems at every turn. That culture – like our technology – is in our heads, not in our hands.

In a world driven by Western science and technology, it is hard to persuade people that the answer is both obvious and available. We don't need to invent something new; we need to recover a relational perspective to each other and to the planet that primitive cultures (to use the anthropological distinction) have never lost. The Old Savage needs to remember the lessons first learned long ago if he's going to live in the New Civilization without destroying it, himself and the planet.

Somehow, in a world that loves to parrot the ideology of progress, this does not seem right. Yet it is the rediscovery of relation that holds the key to a sustainable future for us all. It is found in the universe of values, the importance of which is discounted by the metrics of progress.

The Industrial Revolutions of the last three centuries have made metrical efficiency their hallmark. With every generation, we are "swifter, higher, stronger," as the Olympic motto says. Yet we never ask if we should be, in ethical terms; we never ask what a focus on these metrics says about who we are or what life itself means. The increasing dis-integration of spirit and body in Western culture has meant a focus on one or the other. Values, along with religion and spirituality, are assigned to the realm of the personal, under the assumption that such perspectives contribute little to the metrics of our lives together.

Western science is a powerful tool for understanding some aspects of the universe in which we live, but not all of them. It should not be viewed as an expression of unimpeachable Truth, in order to exempt its methods and results from necessary critique. Even though it has now spread around the world, it carries with it the values, attitudes and ideas of the culture that produced it.

If I say that every culture has discovered and developed the practical knowledge it needed not only to survive, but to thrive, you can see where this is going: There isn't just one way to skin the apple. Ancient cultures accomplished feats of mathematics and engineering that we would hesitate to emulate – and they did it without any of our advantages. There was something in their systems of practical knowledge – of science and technology – that was appropriate to what they needed to do. As long as they made the right choices, as individuals and as cultures, they survived. When they stopped making the right choices, they did not.

The crucial element was not the tools themselves, nor the practical knowledge needed to use them, but the culture itself. Every culture has its blind spot, and when trouble comes from that direction, the solution may be completely obvious to everyone except those in danger. Our blind spot is the metrical universe and the tools we use to manipulate it. Whether we are measuring nature or calculating economies, we set aside the non-metrical universe as irrelevant or consign it to our private lives, where it is no one else's business.

This needs to stop. We need to change the game. We can't calculate a right relationship with the Earth, but we can feel it. We can't commodify and manipulate our connections with other people, but we can create relationships that reflect compassion and care. Time and space do not define a relationship. Nor is chronological age a measure of maturity. Wisdom is a quality, not a quantity. Love can trump logic and does. These statements — and many more – express a view of life and the universe that is not constrained by metrics.

Too many of us don't feel the Earth any more

than we feel our relationships with other people. Loneliness and alienation are the two main themes of an unsustainable culture – a separation from the world in which we live and from the people with whom we live. The consequence is as obvious as the solution is simple: a sustainable future requires us to engage the Earth that lies all around us and to risk a relationship with the people who cross our paths each day.

Perhaps we could simply call it a love of other people and a passion for the planet, but it changes the game. It builds community locally where it counts the most. It recognizes the relations we have with the environment and urges us in the direction of respect instead of exploitation. It gives future generations a voice in our decisions. It guides the choices we make about what technology is appropriate, because those choices are made in relationship with everyone and everything involved. It inspires us to find new ways to solve problems, out of care for each other and the planet instead of out of some compulsion.

We need more passion and less concern for "progress" when it comes to the things that matter for a sustainable future. After all, isolation can only be countered by community. Helplessness disappears when we choose to act, even in small ways, out of what we value – and in acting, we discover that what we value is shared by other people, with whom we can begin to share the relationships that lead to community.

In a world of serious numbers that tabulate everything from climate change to economics to overpopulation, all of this sounds trivial, even trite. Yet it is precisely our lack of relation that leads us to destroy the environment, to place a higher value on present economic returns than future possibilities, to ignore people in favour of supposed profits.

Wherever we create relationships, we undermine the unsustainable culture that tries to turn those relationships into connections, that tries to make money more important than people, that commodifies our feelings into something that can be bought, sold or traded – and even tries to place a number on happiness.

Our best economic and environmental models confront us with the linearity of impending disaster. Unless we change what we do, the outcomes are inevitable. The numbers are serious.

We must do things differently. But the inevitabilities found in these predictions are a product of the same view of life, the universe and other people that created the unsustainable culture that created the problem. It is this culture that has to change – and that is in our heads, not in our hands.

Organic systems are not linear – never have been. People are not linear – never will be. Ecological systems involving people and a planet full of living things are not linear – never could be. Life is not mechanism; value can't be counted. In a universe of relations, more is possible than we can begin to imagine. Other cultures than our own knew this; we have just forgotten that what the universe means is not the same as how it is measured.

At the heart of it all, the universe is Gift. Life itself is Gift. How we share our life with other people and with other living things is our own gift; through what we give, we create relationships that guide the choices we make.

It's a gift, not an exchange. Who we are cannot be counted and measured. The Old Savage needs to be reminded of his humanity, his place in community, his relations with other people, his role in the Earth story. He needs to be reminded of the Turtle's Gift and how it symbolizes the shared bonds among all living creatures. There will always be metrics, things that need to be counted and measured, but the meaning behind those metrics is the key to a sustainable future.

Change the game. Transform the impossible into the improbable — and then make it happen.

For a sustainable future, we need to understand Life and our relations with other people not in terms of economy or exchange, but as Gift – not in expectation of any return, without calculation of cost, but instead as a celebration of Presence with another.

In that moment of Presence, the universe changes in the way all of us need it to change.

Bookshelf

To begin with the Old Savage, Raymond Blaine Fosdick's *The Old Savage in the New Civilization* (New York: Doubleday, Doran and Company, 1928) is readable and still current enough that it should be republished. While little has been written on Fosdick himself, the best item available is still Daryl L. Revoldt's unpublished Ph.D. dissertation, *Raymond Fosdick: Reform, Internationalism, and the Rockefeller Foundation* (University of Akron, May 1982).

Arthur S. Eddington's *The Nature of the Physical World* (New York: Macmillan, 1929) and his Swarthmore Lecture, *Science and the Unseen World* (New York: Macmillan, 1929) are two of his best works from the interwar period. For the context of his ideas on science and religion in that period, see my *ABC of Armageddon: Bertrand Russell on Science, Religion and the Next War,*

1919–1938 (Albany: SUNY Press, 2001). A recent and excellent book on Eddington is Matthew Stanley's *Practical Mystic: Religion, Science, and A. S. Eddington* (Chicago: University of Chicago Press, 2007).

For those interested in exploring the historical development of what we know as modern Western science, Lesley Cormack and Andrew Ede's *A History of Science in Society: From Philosophy to Utility,* 2nd edition (Toronto: University of Toronto Press, 2012) is a careful and useful guide. Looking at the trajectory of science, particularly its popular understanding, Bernard Lightman's *Victorian Popularizers of Science: Designing Nature for New Audiences* (Chicago: University of Chicago Press, 2007) is an excellent foundation for Peter J. Bowler's *Science for All: The Popularization of Science in Early Twentieth-Century Britain* (Chicago: University of Chicago Press, 2009). For historical perspectives on the relationships between science and religion, John Hedley Brooke's *Science and Religion: Some Historical Perspectives* (Cambridge: Cambridge University Press, 1991), coupled with *Reconstructing Nature:*

The Engagement of Science and Religion (with Geoffrey Cantor) (Edinburgh: T & T Clark, 1998), and Peter J. Bowler's *Reconciling Science and Religion: The Debate in Early Twentieth-Century Britain* (Chicago: University of Chicago Press, 2001) build on the earlier classic *God and Nature: Historical Essays on the Encounter between Christianity and Science*, edited by David C. Lindberg and Ronald L. Numbers (Berkeley: University of California Press, 1986).

No one, certainly in Canada, can think about sustainability and the environment without encountering the work of David Suzuki. Among his books (confessing I have read them all), I found these most germane to my current thinking about sustainability: *The Sacred Balance: Rediscovering our Place in Nature* (with Amanda McConnell) (Vancouver: Douglas & McIntyre, 2002); *The Big Picture: Reflections on Science, Humanity, and a Quickly Changing Planet* (with Dave Robert Taylor) (Vancouver: Douglas & McIntyre, 2009); and finally *The Legacy: An Elder's Vision for Our Sustainable Future* (Vancouver: Douglas & McIntyre, 2010).

Amid much excellent scholarship on the

origins of modern science, I have always liked the work of Steven Shapin, not only in the wonderful short book *The Scientific Revolution* (Chicago: University of Chicago Press, 1996), but in its predecessors, *A Social History of Truth: Civility and Science in Seventeenth-Century England* (Chicago: University of Chicago Press, 1994) and the classic *Leviathan and the Air-Pump: Hobbes, Boyle, and the Experimental Life* (with Simon Schaffer) (Princeton; Princeton University Press, 1985).

Toward the end of his life, Thomas Berry's ideas finally appeared in print, notably *The Dream of the Earth* (San Francisco: Sierra Club Books, 1988) and *The Great Work: Our Way into the Future* (New York: Bell Tower, 1999). His earlier essays were edited by Mary Evelyn Tucker, with the best published ones, in my opinion, appearing in *Evening Thoughts: Reflecting on Earth as Sacred Community* (San Francisco: Sierra Club Books, 2006) and *The Sacred Universe: Earth, Spirituality, and Religion in the Twentieth Century* (New York: Columbia University Press, 2009). His work is a continuation of important interdisciplinary thinking that I would trace to

Albert Schweitzer, especially in *The Philosophy of Civilization* (New York: Macmillan, 1949) and in *Out of My Life and Thought: An Autobiography*, translated by C. T. Campion (New York: Henry Holt and Company, 1933).

For an interesting series of reflections on the state of modern science, Western culture and the nature of our unsustainable present, Robert Pirsig's *Zen and the Art of Motorcycle Maintenance* (New York: Bantam) continues to offer as quirky and as thoughtful a perspective today as it did when it was published in 1974. Jane Jacobs's gloomy *Dark Age Ahead* (Toronto; Random House, 2004) was out-gloomed by James Lovelock's *The Vanishing Face of Gaia: A Final Warning* (London: Penguin/Allen Lane, 2009), but both contain serious aspects of "what is given" that need to be understood. For the darker side of Western science, which provides other dimensions to the genial myth of the scientific method, see Evelyn Fox Keller's *Reflections on Gender and Science* (New Haven: Yale University Press, 1985) and Theodore Roszak's *The Gendered Atom: Reflections on the Sexual Psychology of Science* (Berkeley: Conari

Press, 1999), along with Carolyn Merchant's *Radical Ecology: The Search for a Livable World* (New York: Routledge, 1992) – the sequel to her *Death of Nature: Women, Ecology and the Scientific Revolution* (San Francisco: Harper and Row, 1980).

While I take issue with his economic focus, I have appreciated Paul Hawken's *The Ecology of Commerce: A Declaration of Sustainability* (New York: HarperCollins, 1993), which led into his later book (with Amory Lovins and L. Hunter Lovins) *Natural Capitalism: Creating the Next Industrial Revolution* (New York: Little, Brown and Company, 1999). *Blessed Unrest: How the Largest Movement in the World Came into Being and Why No One Saw It Coming* (New York: Viking, 2007) demonstrates the problem with his approach, as other people did see it coming. I have more sympathy with the work of John R. Ehrenfeld in *Sustainability by Design: A Subversive Strategy for Transforming Our Consumer Culture* (New Haven: Yale University Press, 2008), John Bellamy Foster in *The Ecological Revolution: Making Peace with the Planet* (New York: Monthly Review Press,

2009), and Mark Hathaway and Leonardo Boff in *The Tao of Liberation: Exploring the Ecology of Transformation* (Maryknoll, New York: Orbis, 2009).

While more needs to be explored and written about the importance of the gift in history, my thinking has been shaped by David Graeber's *Toward an Anthropological Theory of Value: The False Coin of Our Own Dreams* (New York: Palgrave, 2001), Scott Cutler Shershow's *The Work and the Gift* (Chicago: University of Chicago Press, 2005), and their predecessors, Marshall Sahlins, who wrote *Stone Age Economics* (New York: Aldine de Gruyter, 1972) and Marcel Mauss, for his classic *The Gift: Forms and Functions of Exchange in Archaic Societies*, translated by Ian Cunnison (Glencoe, Illinois: The Free Press, 1954). The most recent work consulted was *Gift and Economy: Ethics, Hospitality and the Market*, edited by Eric R. Severson (Newcastle upon Tyne: Cambridge Scholars Publishing, 2012), which pushes me in the future to consider more of the hermeneutic implications of the gift. The best book I have found on this topic, so far, remains Lewis Hyde's *The Gift:*

Creativity and the Artist in the Modern World (Toronto: Vintage, 2007; originally published in 1983). The Ojibway myth of the Turtle's Gift is drawn from the version in Basil Johnston's *Ojibway Heritage* (Toronto: McClelland and Stewart, 1976).

Saving my favourites for last, there is much that needs to be said about our understanding of technology. There are many good anthologies of classic texts in the philosophy of technology, in addition to which I would highlight Ursula Franklin's 1989 Massey Lectures, *The Real World of Technology,* 2nd edition, revised (Toronto: Anansi, 1999), which I have successfully used in the classroom for many years. Add to her work that of George Grant in *Technology and Justice* (Toronto: Anansi, 1986) and *Technology and Empire: Perspectives on North America* (Toronto: Anansi, 1968), and you will find some of the foundational material for my articles on technology and progress, among other contributions related to sustainability, in the two-volume *Battleground: Science and Technology*, edited with Sal Restivo (Westport, Connecticut: Greenwood, 2008). As friend, colleague and mentor, Sal continues to push the boundaries in his own work and challenges me to do the same.

I am still grateful for Bert Hall's ideas about the social history of technology in relation to the copy of Henry Ford's article on "Mass Production," from *Encyclopedia Britannica*, 13th edition (1926), supp., volume 2, 821–23, which Bert gave me so many years ago, along with much thoughtful advice and support. Trevor H. Levere's compassionate obsession with combining excellence in teaching and scholarship still inspires me as it did when he introduced me to the work of Michael Faraday, to Victorian science, and then to Geoffrey Cantor. I was privileged to hear Cantor's first paper on Faraday, which later led to his important book, *Michael Faraday: Sandemanian and Scientist* (London: Macmillan, 1991), and have appreciated his friendship ever since.

Other Titles in this Series

Digging the City

An Urban Agriculture Manifesto

Rhona McAdam

ISBN 978-1-927330-21-0

Little Black Lies

Corporate & Political Spin
in the Global War for Oil

Jeff Gailus

ISBN 978-1-926855-68-4

The Insatiable Bark Beetle

Dr. Reese Halter

ISBN 978-1-926855-67-7

The Incomparable Honeybee

and the Economics of Pollination
Revised & Updated

Dr. Reese Halter

ISBN 978-1-926855-65-3

The Beaver Manifesto

Glynnis Hood

ISBN 978-1-926855-58-5

The Grizzly Manifesto

In Defence of the Great Bear

by Jeff Gailus

ISBN 978-1-897522-83-7

Becoming Water

Glaciers in a Warming World

Mike Demuth

ISBN 978-1-926855-72-1

Ethical Water

Learning To Value What Matters Most

Robert William Sandford
& Merrell-Ann S. Phare

ISBN 978-1-926855-70-7

Denying the Source

The Crisis of First Nations Water Rights

Merrell-Ann S. Phare

ISBN 978-1-897522-61-5

The Weekender Effect

Hyperdevelopment in Mountain Towns

Robert William Sandford

ISBN 978-1-897522-10-3

RMB saved the following resources by printing the pages of this book on chlorine-free paper made with 100% post-consumer waste:

Trees · 8, fully grown

Water · 3,625 gallons

Energy · 3 million BTUs

Solid Waste · 230 pounds

Greenhouse Gases · 804 pounds

Calculations based on research by Environmental Defense and the Paper Task Force. Manufactured at Friesens Corporation.